Arches National Park

DAYHIKER'S GUIDE

Arches National Park

DAYHIKER'S GUIDE

Jerome and Susan Malitz

Johnson Books
BOULDER

Published by Johnson Books, a subsidiary of Big Earth Publishing,
1880 South 57th Court, Boulder, Colorado 80301. E-mail: books@jpcolorado.com
www.johnsonbooks.com

9 8 7 6 5 4 3 2 1

Cover design: Eric Christensen
Cover photo: Seth Malitz
Author photo: Cathy Bonan-Hamada

Library of Congress Cataloging-in-Publication Data
Malitz, Jerome, 1936–
Arches National Park dayhiker's guide: Utah's slickrock country / Jerome and Suzy Malitz.
p. cm.
Includes bibliographical references and index.
ISBN 1-55566-336-2
1. Hiking—Utah—Arches National Park—Guidebooks. 2. Arches National Park (Utah)—Guidebooks. I. Malitz, Suzy. II. Title
GV199.42.U82A736 2005
796.51'09792'59—dc22 2004023587

Printed in the United States of America

WARNING: Hiking in mountainous terrain can be a high-risk activity. This guidebook is not a substitute for your experience and common sense. The users of this guidebook assume full responsibility for their own safety. Weather, terrain conditions, and individual abilities must be considered before undertaking any of the hikes in this guide.

Contents

Acknowledgments

The authors were fortunate in having had the help of many generous people in preparing this book.

We owe a great debt of gratitude to the officials and volunteers of Arches National Park. To a person, they are knowledgeable, friendly, and extraordinarily helpful. Our special thanks go to Volunteer Ranger Jane Kosut, Ranger Miriam Graham, and Diane Allen, Chief of Interpretation. Their encouragement and enthusiasm were invaluable; their patience with our endless questions went far beyond the call of duty.

Our thanks to David Budd, Professor of Geology at the University of Colorado, for helping us understand the geological dynamics that gave rise to the Park.

Our thanks to Alan Wilson, whose father Bates was superintendent of the Park from 1949 to 1964. Alan grew up in Moab and shared many experiences in the Park with his father. Hearing him tell of these experiences gave us some sense of what the Park was like half a century ago.

Special thanks go to Cathy and Ed Bonan-Hamada, professors of mathematics at Mesa State College. They accompanied us on many of the hikes, contributed several of the photographs, and offered invaluable suggestions to improve the text.

To all of these kind and generous people—many thanks for your help.

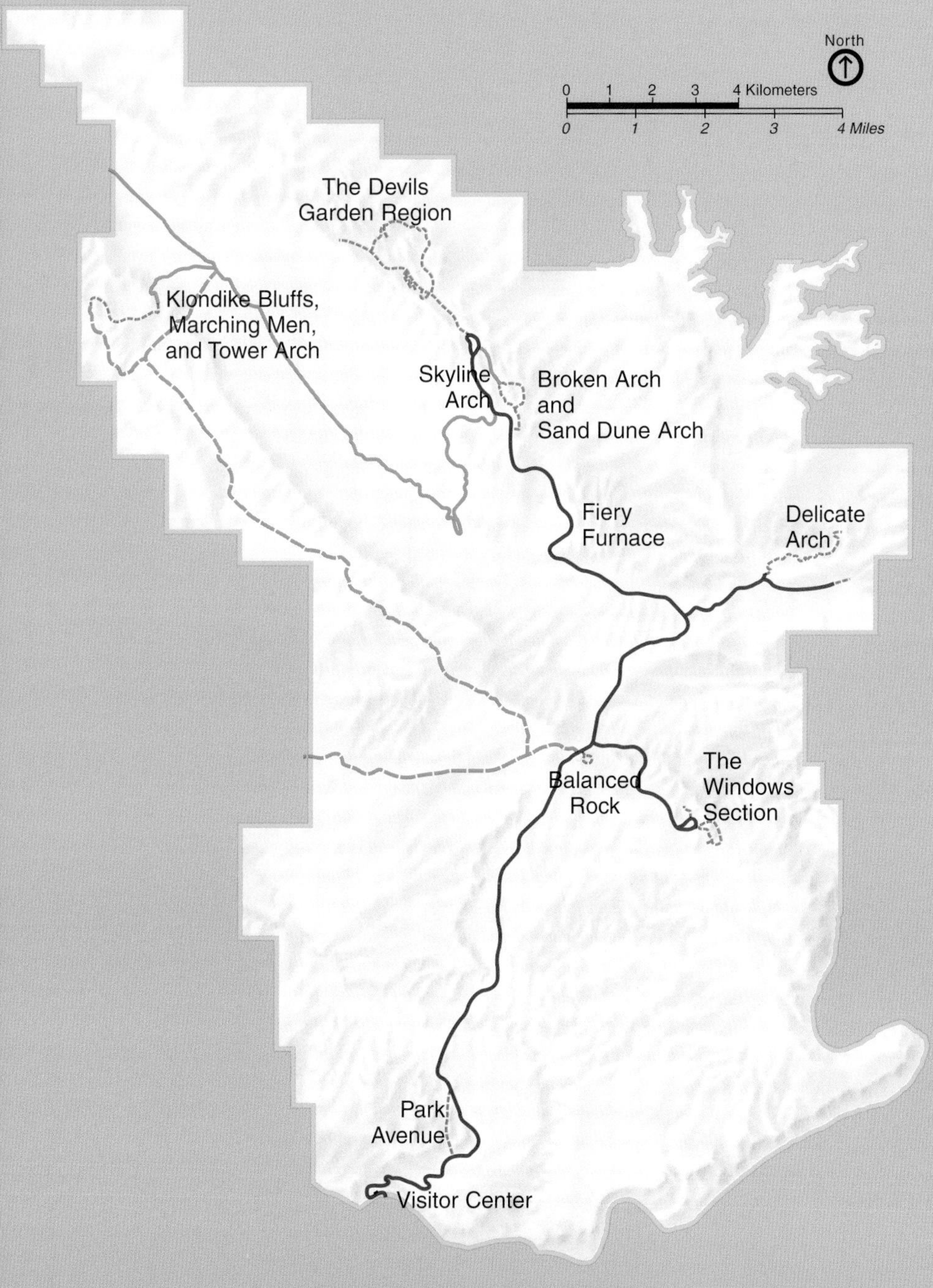
North
0 1 2 3 4 Kilometers
0 1 2 3 4 Miles
The Devils
Garden Region
Klondike Bluffs,
Marching Men,
and Tower Arch
Skyline
Arch
Broken Arch
and
Sand Dune Arch
Fiery
Furnace
Delicate
Arch
Balanced
Rock
The
Windows
Section
Park
Avenue
Visitor Center

Arches National Park

PART I
About the Park

Introduction

In an area of only 119 square miles in east-central Utah, Nature has created a grand sculpture court of extraordinary formations. Some are so fanciful that they have earned names such as Park Avenue, Fiery Furnace, Devils Garden, and Parade of Elephants. Some are so massive that you might think that they would survive unchanged forever. Others are so large and yet so delicately proportioned that it's a wonder that they don't crash to the ground as you watch.

There are monoliths, towers, enormous walls, pinnacles, and of course arches—more than 2,000 of them—including Delicate Arch, the Park's signature piece, and Landscape Arch, the world's longest, spanning 306 feet (over 90 m).

In spite of their monumental scale, some of the forms can be approached to within neck-straining closeness and many within arm's length. You can climb up onto several of the arches, walk atop some of the giant sandstone walls, and play hide-and-seek among some of the columns.

Not all of the Park's features are on a colossal scale. There are many smaller attractions that are fascinating in measure far exceeding their size.

The region is famous for its flora—often both strange and beautiful at the same time. There are flowers so exquisitely delicate that they seem out of place in this unforgiving, rough-hewn landscape of rock and sand. Not only do they seem out of place in the desert, but even on the very plants that bear them—plants that are often thorny and so sparsely furnished with such small leaves as to appear lifeless. Yet in season, and the season is a long one, they set pockets in the desert ablaze with vibrant color.

Even the stone from which the arches, fins, and other giant features of the Park were sculpted holds special interest when seen up close. Some surfaces are lavishly embossed, others boldly patterned in bas-relief. Still others are delicately washed with exotic minerals, filigreed with lichens, or painted with glistening desert varnish—all part of the patina of time. Different rock types and mineral deposits give the rocks gradations of colors and patterns that often make them seem more like fine tapestry than rock.

The fauna, too, is remarkable, and some of it a bit scary. Birds and butterflies abound, but there are also some nasties. Poisonous snakes and scorpions, for instance, can be found in the Park. While far from common, one should be aware of their presence.

Penstemon

Lupine

Opuntia Cactus

Prickly Poppy

Balsamroot

Scarlet Mallow

Prince's Plume

Sand Verbena

Aster

Yucca

Most of the Park's magnificent scenery is readily accessible. There are easy, short walks and some more challenging treks. But for the most part, the trails are family friendly. Traveling them is neither difficult nor hazardous, so full attention can be given to the beauty and wonder of this place—Arches National Park.

What Follows

Experiencing this fantastic landscape, one cannot help but wonder: How did it arise? What forces brought it into being? What is the nature of the materials that permitted such wondrous constructions? How will time continue to sculpt this landscape?

In "The Story of the Stone," we outline some of the current ideas about the geological dynamics that gave rise to the incredible land forms we see here today.

In "Human History," we discuss the human presence in the region, the culture and beliefs of the native peoples who lived here long ago, and the story of the more recent settlers who lived here in the last couple of centuries. This astonishing region is not designed to supply creature comforts, at least not to creatures of our own kind. However, it is easy to believe that the region had a profound and spiritual hold on those who came to visit. Many stayed, captured by the mystical aspect of the place, rather than its physical amenities.

Desert country is usually inhospitable. In "An Ounce of Prevention," we describe some of the risks that the hiker might encounter in this region. Arches National Park, with its well-maintained main road and hiking trails, welcomes visitors, but a bit of forethought and planning will do much to guarantee a safe and rewarding visit.

"Deserving of Your Respect" discusses ecological concerns and seeks to foster good stewardship of the land within Arches National Park.

In "Visitor Center," we encourage you to make use of the resources available to Park visitors. The Visitor Center is a great place to start your adventure.

The remainder of the book is devoted to trail descriptions that tell you how to get to where you want to go and to photos that illustrate the main features along the trail, as well as at the trail's end. A bibliography and index conclude the book.

The Story of the Stone

Finding yourself in Arches National Park—surrounded by gigantic stone formations, at once majestic, beautiful, and bizarre—you cannot help but wonder how such a landscape came to be. Cliffs, canyons, fins, spires, and arches—fabulous arches in greater concentration than anywhere else on the planet. How were they formed? What titanic forces, what inexorable processes forged this region into the enormous sculpture court that we see today? How long did it take? And how will it proceed?

The geologic history of this region is still being crafted, a work in progress. New pieces of the puzzle are unearthed, literally, year by year, and the story is continually being fleshed out. Details are added, and minor themes are revised. Sometimes even major theories are reworked or added, as was the case in the early 1970s when, supported by a preponderance of evidence, tectonic plate theory and its offshoot, continental drift, finally received general acceptance.

The earth's surface was no longer viewed as an array of immovable continents, with the configuration essentially unchanged since taking shape on the crust of a cooling, molten sphere that formed some 4.6 billion years ago. Instead, the new theory argues that the crust is partitioned into pieces, called tectonic plates, and that these plates can move independently of each other, as they float on the core of liquid magma.

In fact, it is now thought that at one time there was only one landmass, the supercontinent Pangea. About 180 million years ago, Pangea fissured into several pieces, and then these pieces began to drift apart, forming the continents of today. Even a fan of jigsaw puzzles might find it a challenge to piece together the continents into a single landmass, and geologists still entertain several alternative reconstructions. Key evidence of continental drift is found in the similarity of the geological strata along the presumed lines of attachment of the continents. Fossil evidence of similar life forms also bolsters the theory.

Understanding that these plates move—that they crumple, fissure, collide, and slide under one another—provides the conceptual foundation for understanding how the earth's surface has evolved and how it will continue to evolve. Giant rifts form canyons. Abutting plates buckle upward to form mountain ranges. One plate sliding over another fosters volcanism. A landmass once temperate can be translocated to the equator or from the equator to another region. Upheavals can drain seas; a declining region can usher them back.

While the shifting of tectonic plates provides the grand dynamic that shapes the continents, other forces and processes further sculpt the earth's surface features. Flowing water carves canyons. Frozen into moving glaciers, water sculpts valleys. Combined with CO_2 in the atmosphere, water falls as weak carbonic acid—perfect for dissolving limestone and the calcite that binds sand into sandstone. Water expands upon freezing, so when water is trapped in rock fissures over winter, it forms a network of ice wedges that pry the stone apart.

Windblown sand abrades and polishes stone. Creatures of the sea extract lime out of the water and build reefs and islands out of limestone. Sediments accumulate and solidify. Even solid rock deforms when subjected

Moab Fault as seen near the start of the main road.

to enough pressure. All of these forces and processes continue inexorably to change the face of the planet.

The region that is now Utah was once located at the equator. Plate tectonics lowered the surface in some parts and forced uplifts in other parts of the region. Mountain ranges rose and later were eroded away. During some periods of time, mountain ranges partly bordered broad valleys, forming enormous basins. A vast sea intruded into the region, then retreated, and was sealed off and evaporated. The cycle was repeated over and over again. In one 10 to 15 million-year period alone, the cycle was repeated twenty-nine times.

Each retreat of the sea left behind salt. Salt was deposited on salt—to a depth of as much as 10,000 feet (350 m) in some places.

Then about 300 million years ago, the incursions by the sea abated, and the vast basin of salt began to be covered by debris. Debris came in from nearby mountain ranges, products of erosion. Stream and lake deposits contributed to the buildup. Desert sands added to the crust. And the crust thickened to nearly a mile (1.61 km) in depth. Since the debris comprising the crust came from different sources at different times, the crust was not homogenous, but layered. Some layers were weakly cemented and so were easily eroded, while other layers were more resistant to erosion.

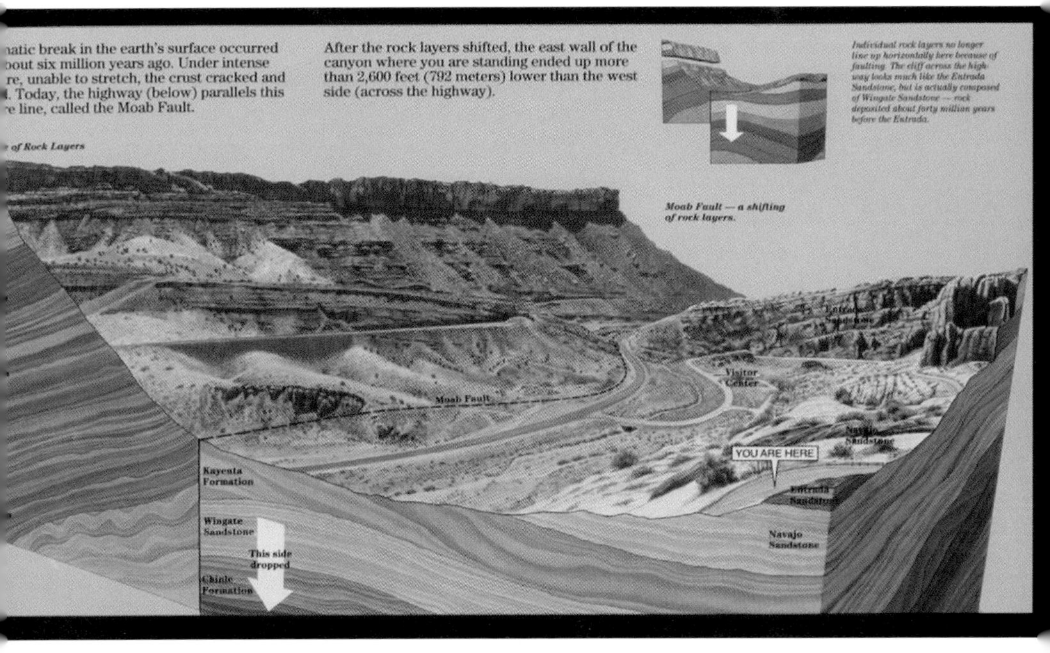

Moab Fault, informative placard.

Stone regatta—fins in Devils Garden.

A mass of salt is deformable under pressure. Under its covering of stone, the salt deposits in the region of Arches National Park began to flow. In places it flowed over uplifts and worn-down mountain ranges, forming elongated mounds (anticlines), oriented with their long axis running northwest to southeast.

The rock crust covering the salt bent over the anticlines. This bending of the crust caused parallel fissures to form in the stone, the fissures running in the direction of the long axis of the anticlines. Erosion by wind-driven sand, rain, and most of all running water widened the fissures. The thick flanges of stone between the fissures became narrower as their sides were worn away.

What remains of those flanges are called fins, and there are many examples of them to be seen in the Park. A fleet of these stone schooners in parallel formation on the desert floor is an impressive sight, one to remember. Not only are the fins wondrous in their own right, but these are the structures within which the famed arches formed.

How is an arch created? Wear-away or chip-away the rock on the side of a fin and continue until you reach the other side. This occurs more quickly near the bottom of the fins, in relatively soft layers of stone. There are two main processes by which erosion does its work, and the two processes work independently at times and collaboratively in others. The more dramatic process is thought to be the least common—large chunks of rock are loosened from the fin and fall free of it. More commonly, the rock is gradually eroded into sand and gravel as acid rain dissolves binding material.

The processes are ongoing today and will continue into the future. You can see all stages of arch formation and arch destruction in the Park. In the Windows Section, you can see a mighty arch in the making. There is a huge concavity in the side of a fin, not yet perforating it. Small perforations—"windows," they are called—are common; they need to attain a minimum diameter of three feet (.91 m) before they are accorded arch status.

When an arch collapses—and they will all collapse in time—they leave behind two walls in tandem or even two isolated spires, as will be the case when Delicate Arch loses its top.

Nascent arch—Windows section.

And someday, Arches National Park will be no more—eroded away, covered over, deformed by plate tectonics, and rendered invisible or transformed into something entirely different. Will another version of Arches National Park arise nearby or elsewhere? Some geologists believe so, but others point to the unique conditions that gave rise to the formations in this Park and argue that it is highly unlikely that anything like it will ever form again.

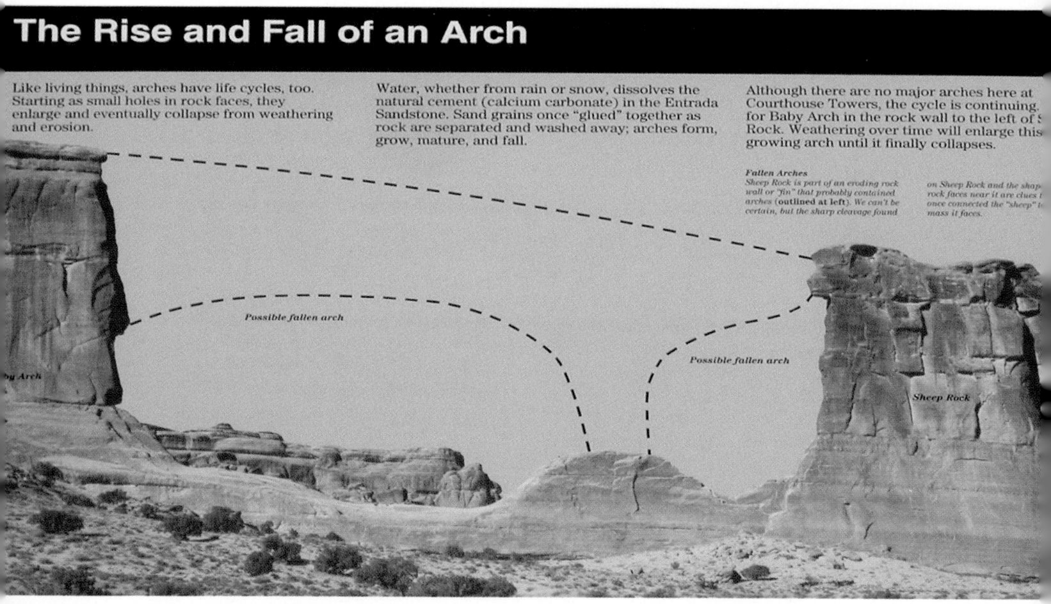

The Rise and Fall of an Arch
Like living things, arches have life cycles, too. Starting as small holes in rock faces, they enlarge and eventually collapse from weathering and erosion.
Water, whether from rain or snow, dissolves the natural cement (calcium carbonate) in the Entrada Sandstone. Sand grains once "glued" together as rock are separated and washed away; arches form, grow, mature, and fall.
Although there are no major arches here at Courthouse Towers, the cycle is continuing for Baby Arch in the rock wall to the left of
Rock. Weathering over time will enlarge this growing arch until it finally collapses.
Fallen Arches
Sheep Rock is part of an eroding rock wall or "fin" that probably contained arches (outlined at left). We can't be certain, but the sharp cleavage found
on Sheep Rock and the
rock faces near it are
once connected the "sheep"
mass it faces.
Possible fallen arch
Possible fallen arch
Sheep Rock

Interpretive placard—the demise of an arch.

Human History

The archeological record of the Arches National Park area is scant, but there is evidence that there were people in the region 12,000 years ago. The climate was quite different then—cooler and with much more moisture. Vegetation was abundant, and animals as large as mammoth, longhaired bison, and giant ground sloth roamed the land. Early human inhabitants found an abundance of game and edible plants, and they survived for thousands of years as hunters and gatherers.

But the climate changed, gradually becoming warmer and drier. Plant populations also changed, and edible plants were harder to find. Many of the game animals were no longer available, driven elsewhere in search of food or driven to extinction by overhunting. The people who relied primarily on hunting and gathering found it increasingly difficult to survive. They apparently left the region around 2,000 B.C., but other people moved in, people who used agriculture to supplement wild foods.

There are several sites in today's Arches National Park where one can see signs of these ancient cultures—pictographs (rock paintings), petroglyphs (drawings scratched into desert varnish), and sites where chalcedony was quarried for making tools and weapons. Some of these artifacts date back 2,000 years, but most are only centuries old.

No one knows for sure when Euro-Americans first made contact with the native-Americans in this region, but we do know that hunters and trappers were plying their trade there by the mid-1800s. An inscription carved into the base of a fin in Arches National Park reads, "Dennis Julien, June 9, 1844."

In 1855, Mormons established the Elk Mountain Mission in Moab Valley, but the post was abandoned in September of the same year after three of the missionaries were killed by local Utes.

In 1888, John Wesley Wolfe and his son moved from Ohio and set up a ranch near what is now the main trailhead to Delicate Arch. A nearby spring provided enough water for a few cows and a small garden. John was a Civil War veteran, and his government pension supplemented his homesteading. In 1907, John's daughter, her husband, and their two children moved to the ranch. After a flash flood destroyed the original cabin, the family built a new one, along with a root cellar. These structures are still to be seen today. In 1910, the Wolfe family sold the ranch and moved back to

Ohio. The ranch changed ownership several more times before being purchased by the federal government.

Over the decades that followed, many people visited the area and were so impressed by what they saw that they lobbied for its protection. Alexander Ringhoffer, a prospector who traveled through the region in the 1920s, has been accorded the title "Father of Arches National Park." His pleas for the public protection of the region eventually came to the attention of Stephen T. Mather, the first director of the National Park Service. Mather was soon convinced that the area deserved public protection, and he pushed for the creation of a national monument.

Finally, in 1929, Herbert Hoover signed the bill that set aside a mere seven square miles (11.3 sq km) as Arches National Monument. Even that puny acreage was deemed too generous by the Eisenhower administration, and they diminished its size. President Lyndon Johnson expanded it to 114 square miles (184 sq km). In 1971 President Richard Nixon accorded the area national park status. And in 1998, under President William Clinton, the Park was enlarged once again and now encompasses 119 square miles (192 sq km).

Wolfe Ranch dating back to 1900.

An Ounce of Prevention

In spite of its inhospitable appearance, Arches National Park is generally a friendly place, but keep in mind that longer trails provide a true back-country experience. Should assistance be needed, it may be more than a mile away, and cell phones are unreliable in some areas of the Park. So, a bit of caution, common sense, and preparation are warranted and will go far in assuring a safe and rewarding visit.

What follows is a brief overview of some of the more common hazards that may be encountered. However, this chapter is not a substitute for a first-aid manual. There are several good manuals that are currently available, and every hiker should carry one.

1. From mid-spring to mid-fall, heat and sun pose the main threats, and they can conspire to ruin your day or even your entire trip.

Very hot weather and inadequate intake of fluids and salt can result in heat exhaustion. The symptoms may include pale, clammy skin, headache, vomiting, and muscle cramps. The person may feel faint and sick. Urine may be highly colored, with infrequent and unproductive urination. Unchecked, heatstroke may follow.

Give the person fluids to drink. Some food may be taken to help replace lost salt, but salt tablets are too concentrated. Move the person to the coolest nearby place. Drench clothing in cold water if you can, and apply cold or cool compresses to the head, neck, armpits, and joints.

Heatstroke (or sunstroke), a consequence of prolonged exposure to heat, disables the body's temperature controls, and temperature can rapidly rise to 104° F (40° C) or even more. The person's skin becomes hot, dry, and flushed. Pulse is rapid. Confusion and unconsciousness quickly follow. Proceed with the treatment for heat exhaustion, above, and seek help as soon as possible.

Of course, prevention is the wisest course of action. The recommendation that .75 to one quart (about .75 to one liter) of water be allotted for every hour on the trail can be used only as a rough guide. Some persons can get away with less, but others require more. Let caution be your guide.

However, it is possible to take in too much water and deplete the body's salts. The resulting condition is called hyponatremia, and if not recognized and treated in time, it can result in seizures, coma, and death. Initial symptoms are very much like those of heat exhaustion, except that the person has been drinking enough water, urination is productive, and the urine is not highly colored. In the early stages, withhold water and encourage eating. Later stages require medical help as soon as possible.

2. During most of the day, few trails provide shade, and sunburn is a significant threat. Again the effects are insidious; a reddening of the skin, local warming, and maybe a bit of swelling are early signs. There may be systemic symptoms, including nausea, headache, and loss of appetite. Then, depending on the degree of exposure, pain, itching, and blistering can occur. Severe cases require medical attention.

At the earliest signs, take shelter from the sun; move into shade, if you can find some, or at least cover up. Later, analgesic creams can help blunt the itching and pain, and moisturizing creams are soothing and might speed healing.

Again, treatment is much more troublesome than prevention. Use generous amounts of sunscreen with a high SPF (Sun Protection Factor) number, 40 or higher, and UV (ultraviolet light) protection. Apply as needed, especially if sweating. Wear protective clothing: a sun hat, perhaps a light scarf, maybe a long-sleeved shirt, and long pants or a skirt. Keep in mind that some materials are far more protective than others. Of course, these recommendations run contrary to the urge to dress lightly for a hike in the desert heat, but a bit of inconvenience at the beginning of a hike can avert major discomfort later on.

In this land of bare rock, sand, and skies that are usually brilliantly clear, sun glare is not just annoying, it can cause damage to the retina. Sunglasses and a hat with a visor will contribute to your comfort and protect your vision.

3. Too much heat and sun are the most serious threats in desert country, but temperatures can drop quickly after sunset, snow and ice can be encountered in some seasons, and wind is common. A loss of body temperature, hypothermia, is quite possible. Exhaustion, hunger, and thirst are predisposing factors. The elderly and ill are more susceptible. Symptoms include shivering, lack of coordination, and disorientation. Allowed to progress unchecked, coma and death can follow.

At the first sign of hypothermia, give the person small amounts of high-energy food and something warm to drink. Remove wet clothing and bundle up the person in dry clothing. Cover the neck and head. Keep the person moving and take them to a warmer place as soon as possible.

4. Hiking along established trails carries little danger of getting lost. Most of the trails described in this book are clearly marked and easy to follow. Often, there are enough people following the same route as to leave little doubt as to the direction. However, there are a few exceptions. For instance, the Park does not recommend hiking through the Fiery Furnace unless accompanied by a guide, since the maze of canyons there can quickly become disorienting. Ranger-guided tours are available from April through October, but you need to sign up for them at the Visitor Center. During the busiest time of the year, it's a good idea to sign up several days in advance.

Hiking off-trail or along some long trails alone can be dangerous if you get an injury that immobilizes you. Help may be a long time in coming. If you do hike alone, inform a responsible person where you're going and when you expect to return. Notify that person when you do return.

5. Some creatures native to the area pose a threat, but serious injury from them is highly unlikely. Sand fleas, gnats, and harvester ants can be a bother, but these are minor nuisances, usually easy to avoid. Full bloom in the desert brings with it a bounty of bees and wasps. People who have severe reactions to their stings might want to carry an epipen (a spring-loaded hypodermic of epinephrine, available by prescription).

There are tarantulas that roam the desert floor, but these giant, hairy spiders are more fascinating than dangerous, and you should count yourself lucky if you see one. If you do find one, leave it alone. They can deliver a painful bite, and when provoked, they have the nasty habit of rubbing their abdomens with their hind legs, thereby dislodging and launching harpoon-like hairs into the air. Pointed and barbed, these hairs are designed to stick and stay—stick and stay in the membranes of the nose, mouth, or eyes—causing an irritation definitely to be avoided.

There are also several species of scorpions in the area, some poisonous, others not. Those that are can give you a nasty sting, the site of which will become painful and swollen. So, it's best to leave them alone. Scorpions, too, are reclusive and not disposed to attack you.

In addition, there are rattlesnakes in the area that can deliver a dangerous bite. They are also generally secretive and non-aggressive, and an encounter with one is highly unlikely.

Opinions vary as to what is the best treatment for the bite of a rattler, but most agree that the victim should be kept as calm as possible. The limb (if the bite is on a leg or arm) should be kept on the same plane as the heart. Elevating the limb above the level of the heart will cause the venom to be distributed through the body too quickly. Lowering the limb below the level of the heart will slow dissipation of the poison too much and increase the rate of swelling. Seek help as soon as possible, since the administration of antivenum is likely to be the most effective treatment and is most safely administered by trained health professionals.

It is no longer recommended that a tourniquet be applied or that incisions be made at the site of the fang marks. Nor is it recommended that suction by mouth be applied to the wound area in an attempt to remove the poison. Snake bite kits are available that include suction devices. Comprehensive and up-to-date information is available on-line at several web sites.

Not found in the Park are the notorious sidewinder rattler, the western diamondback rattler, or the gila monster. Fortunately, these nasties prefer more southwesterly regions.

6. Falls, scrapes, and bruises are always possible. Although most of the trails are easy to negotiate and few have significant exposure, remember that slickrock is really slick rock, especially when wet or covered by ice and snow. Sand or gravel atop rock can also set you up for a misstep. A good pair of hiking shoes or boots will help you avoid a bruised or twisted ankle and maybe a serious fall.

7. Yes, the desert does get rain, and thunderstorms can be fierce and sudden. Flash flooding is a remote possibility, but when you're in a canyon or between fins, it may be prudent to move to higher ground, even if the storm is miles away. When lightning threatens, avoid exposed terrain, shallow caves, and proximity to metal or tall objects.

8. Finally, watch out for traffic! Drivers are often watching for a glimpse of wildlife, a convenient parking space, or the scenery in general. Being run over by a car is likely to put a damper on your entire visit.

On the other hand, take care when you're doing the driving. The first few miles from the Park entrance is a fairly steep climb with traverses that have a drop-off on one side and close proximity to a stone wall on the other. Once past this stretch, watch out for wildlife, particularly the human kind. These are the kind who are likely to dash across the road or step back onto it in order to compose a photo. Let's hope Darwin isn't watching.

Other than these few risks, most of which are easily avoided, the Park is a friendly place, offering a unique and wondrous landscape to be enjoyed fully and safely with a minimum of concern.

Deserving of Your Respect

Arches National Park is not just a national treasure, it's a treasure belonging to all people. Visitors come from around the world to see this fantastic landscape, and few leave unmoved by the wonder of it.

At first glance, the Park seems indestructible. After all, it is made mostly out of sand and stone, and its creation has to be measured in geologic time—thousands of millions of years. But the Park can be damaged, can be defaced, can be violated.

Vandals have used paint and ink to leave their mark on the walls. Others carved their names into arches and spires. As incomprehensible as it may seem, in 1980 someone threw acid onto a pictograph dating back 1,000 years. While such depredation is not frequent, the Park regularly suffers all too many insults. This Park is ours, at least in stewardship, and so we suffer the insults by extension, as do all future generations.

We can't fathom the mindset of the vandals. Why do they travel to the Park in the first place? Why do they spend the money and time required? Why do they expend the energy to hike the trails? What do they expect to find? What is it that irks them so that it kindles such reprehensible (indeed, criminal) behavior?

Not all insults to the Park are delivered by hoodlums. Some damage is done by decent sorts in an unthinking moment or out of carelessness or ignorance. An unusual plant or flower is seen nearby, picked in order to examine it more closely, and then discarded on the trail to wither in the sun. Beer bottles, soda cans, and food containers light enough to pack in when full, prove too burdensome to carry out when empty. And signs that request visitors to stay on the paths are ignored at the expense of one of the most crucial and fragile components of this desert ecosystem, the cryptobiotic soil.

The desert sand is home to a variety of primitive life forms—algae, fungi, mosses, bacteria, and cyanobacteria. These organisms lace the upper layers of the sand and form a visible crust over much of the surface. The crust binds the sand together and helps to prevent it from being blown away. It also provides nutrients for the higher plants. These primitive organisms form a reddish gray, crumbly surface coating on the sand—humble in appearance, but crucial to the ecology of the Park.

This is the cryptobiotic soil, and it is exceedingly fragile and painfully slow to regenerate. This is why it is so important to heed the signs and stay on the paths.

Even with the best intentions and well-meaning cooperation of visitors, the Park will be under enormous stress in the years ahead. It is becoming increasingly difficult to protect its essential character for future generations, while at the same time accommodating all the visitors who want to see it.

Since early in the 1980s, visitation has been increasing at an alarming rate. In 2002, the Park received over three-quarters of a million visitors. We are loving this Park to death. There is no question that the experience of visiting the Park has changed over time. The solitude that contributes so much to the appreciation of the majestic beauty of the Park is harder and harder to find.

Of course, the spectacular scenery remains, and it will always provide great pleasure to those privileged to see it. Let's do what we can to protect that privilege for future generations.

Cryptobiotic soil—alive with organisms crucial to the ecology of the region.

PART II
The Grand Tour

Visitor Center and the wall you traverse by car to begin exploring the Park.

Visitor Center

Trail 1 is the Desert Nature Trail, a .2-mile loop located at the Visitor Center.

Welcome to Arches National Park. After purchasing your pass at the entrance station, you're ready to head up the side of the plateau and start the tour. However, if you're a first-time visitor, bridle your enthusiasm and drop by the Visitor Center. It will be time well spent and will help you get the most out of your visit.

The Visitor Center is not very large and can be quite crowded. (A new and larger facility is under construction and expected to open in 2005.) Be patient, the Park personnel, rangers and volunteers, are eager to help you. They want to make your stay in the Park as safe and rewarding as possible. Always friendly, courteous, and knowledgeable, they will give you the latest weather information and tell you about the current trail and road conditions. Let them know what you would like to do and your time constraints, and they'll recommend the hikes that will best suit your needs. They'll tell you about the ranger-guided tours and upcoming events, and they will sign you up for the famous hike through Fiery Furnace.

The Visitor Center has a small auditorium where you can watch a video on the Park. It's an engaging, informative presentation, and the photography is marvelous.

The Visitor Center sells books about the region in general and the Park in particular—books about geology, about the plants and animals of the region, and about the region's human history. There are maps, postcards, and souvenirs for sale. Food and beverages, except for water, are not available.

There are toilets in back of the building. Keep in mind that only a few places in the Park have toilets: the trailheads at Balanced Rock, The Windows Section, Delicate Arch, Fiery Furnace, Klondike Bluffs, and Devils Garden. Only the last has drinking water.

Adjoining the Visitor Center is a small but interesting and informative garden. The plants in this garden, all native to the Park, are fascinating in their adaptation to the desert environment. Most of the plants are labeled, and a bit of time spent in the garden will help you identify some of the plants you will find on your hikes.

Before you leave the garden, notice the spectacular cliff behind it to the north. You'll soon be driving up that cliff to reach the plateau, and that's where the adventure begins.

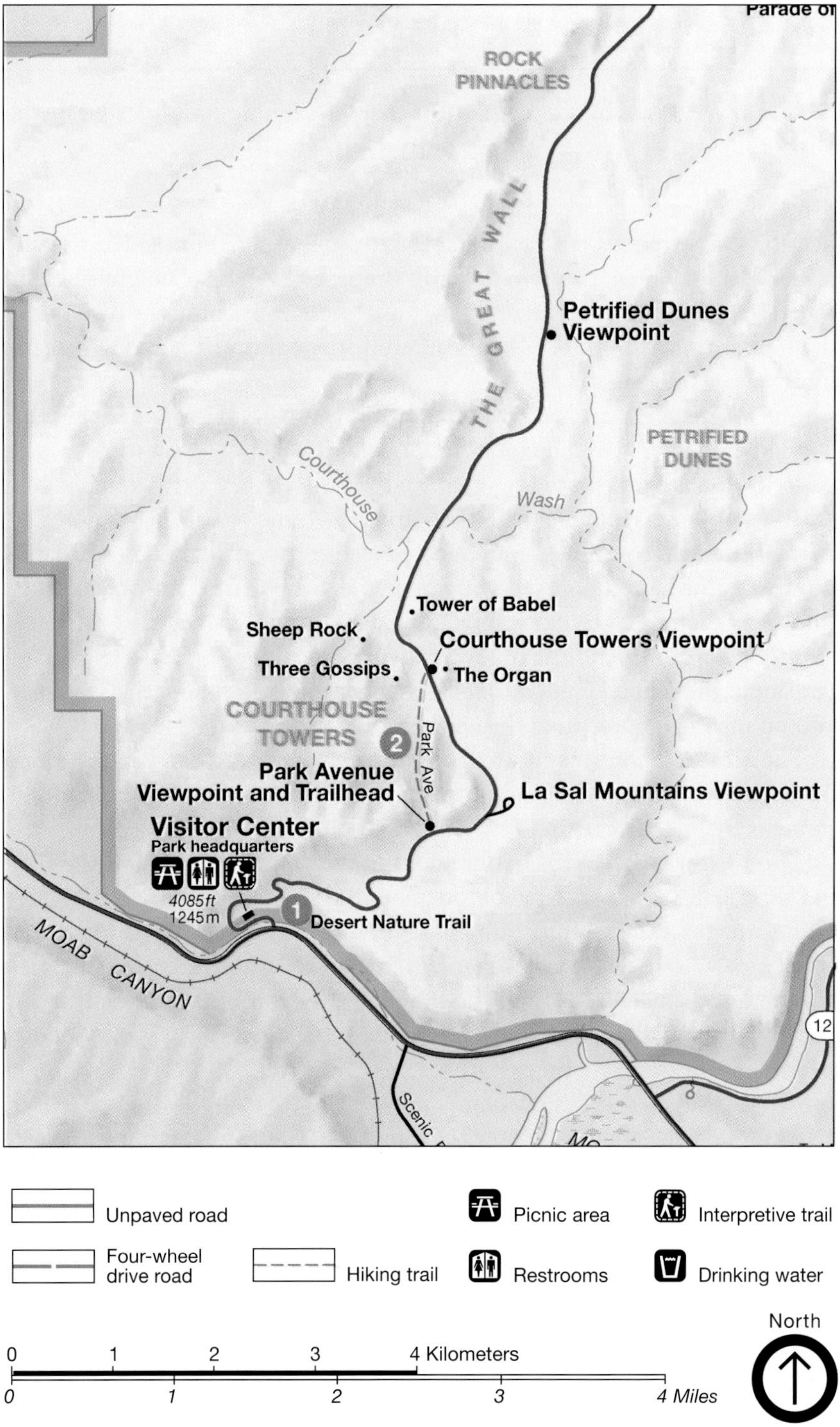
Parade of
ROCK PINNACLES
THE GREAT WALL
Petrified Dunes Viewpoint
PETRIFIED DUNES
Courthouse
Wash
Tower of Babel
Sheep Rock
Courthouse Towers Viewpoint
Three Gossips
The Organ
COURTHOUSE TOWERS
2
Park Ave
Park Avenue Viewpoint and Trailhead
La Sal Mountains Viewpoint
Visitor Center
Park headquarters
4085ft
1245m
1
Desert Nature Trail
MOAB CANYON
12
Scenic
Unpaved road
Four-wheel drive road
Hiking trail
Picnic area
Restrooms
Interpretive trail
Drinking water
0
1
2
3
4 Kilometers
0
1
2
3
4 Miles
North

Park Avenue — Trail 2

Start:	Park Avenue parking area, 2.5 miles (4 km) from the Visitor Center, on the left; or Courthouse Towers parking area, 3.7 miles (6 km) from the Visitor Center, on the right.
Distance:	1 mile (1.6 km) one way.
Elevation gain:	320 feet (98 m) including stairs.
Difficulty:	Moderate.

Lacking the glitz and glitter of its Big Apple namesake, this Park Avenue offers instead a natural promenade lined on each side by vertical walls of stone, rising to a height of between 200 and 300 feet (61 and 91 m). Those who walk this avenue won't be swallowed up by the see-nothing frenetic pace of its eastern counterpart, but instead will experience the monumental grandeur of Nature's architecture.

It's more than the grand scale that captures the imagination. It's the balance and harmony, the proportions and strong lines that distinguish this version. It's too bad that our city avenues so often lack the design coherence of this model. But that's what makes this landscape so special—grandeur without conceit, harmony without contrivance, integrity without arrogance.

Park Avenue is the first major feature that one sees after entering the Park. Given its popularity, the parking area is not overly generous, and peak-season use might require you to queue up for a space.

Some of the most dramatic views of Park Avenue are to be had right from the parking area. From here you have an overview of the avenue far below and the gigantic vertical slabs—Nature's version of skyscrapers—that define its boundaries. This landscape is magnificent at any time of the day, but in the early morning, when the west-facing wall is in shadow, Park Avenue is at its dramatic best.

Don't shortchange yourself by dallying too long in the parking lot. Park Avenue has far more to offer the visitor than that view, as spectacular as it is. To get a much fuller grasp of this magnificent canyon, you have to descend to its floor. A stairway of about thirty stairs leads down from the parking lot. In places the stairs are wide enough to easily accommodate two people side-by-side; in other places, there is barely enough room for one. Take care! There may be gravel on some of the stairs—Nature's ball bearings.

As you begin the descent, look to the wall on your left. There, on the rim, sits a bust of Queen Nefertiti. At least it's a pretty good approximation of the one at the Berlin Museum. Watch your step, but do try to take in the view that unfolds as you descend.

As the walls rise above you, take note of the contrast between the pock-marked, weather-beaten section of the walls and the smooth portions streaked vertically with desert varnish and horizontally by a subtle layering of different rocks. The colors are vivid at midday and even more so in early morning or late afternoon.

The path along this grand avenue is broad and mostly level. Huge slabs of stone form the walkway. Sometimes the pieces are fitted together with such precision that it is obvious that they were adjacent parts of a still larger slab. In other places, generous seams separate the plates, and these seams are often crammed with plants. In still other places, plates are staggered to form a gentle staircase, each broad stair only a few inches thick. The entire scene

Park Avenue from the parking area.

Queen Nefertiti. Not a bad facsimile of the sculpted bust in the Berlin Museum.

Queen Nefertiti in the Berlin Museum.

Along Park Avenue.

often seems more like the product of thoughtful, orderly design, rather than the random workings of nature.

On each side of the path are monumental walls, monoliths, and towers—grand architecture. The avenue even has its side streets, convoluted canyons that meander and vanish in the distance. All along the path are smaller features, whose interest and beauty far exceed their size: waterpocket folds, miniature oases, delicately filigreed flagstones, and pancake-stacks of stone slabs crazily tilted. Here, instead of storefront after storefront displaying the very latest in must-have inconsequentials, you are treated to a gallery of natural gardens—bermed gardens, gardens contained in huge sandstone planters, and surreal gardens whose plants seem to be growing out of solid rock.

On the sand and among the rocks, you find a variety of extraordinary plants in season. At first, the abundance and floriferousness will surprise you. After all, this is desert country. But this garden is located in a wash, an area where water collects from the surrounding rock and flows through the canyon. And the rock moderates temperature and offers some shade. So, all in all, this is a plant-friendly place.

Park Avenue has its side streets.

Tapestry in rock.

Stone staircase along Park Avenue.

There are too many plants to mention here, but you will probably notice the dwarfed and twisted Utah juniper, as picturesque as bonsai. The silvery white sage appears covered with hoarfrost, even on the hottest day. And when in bloom, you can't help but see the waist-high spikes of yucca studded with ivory bells. The four inch (10 cm), bright yellow daisies smothering the two-foot (.6-m) mounds of balsamroot, the extravagant display of orange-to-red globe mallow blossoms on a profusion of two-foot (.6-m) stems, and the three-foot (.9-m) yellow spikes of prince's plume are but part of the bewildering abundance.

Several of these plants are now commercially available and have become all the rage for xeriscape gardens. As apt and wonderful as they are for this application, seeing them here, growing in the wild, is even more satisfying.

As you continue to walk the length of Park Avenue, the path becomes wider, and the great walls on each side begin to step down to the desert floor. Sheep Rock comes into view, while Courthouse Towers looms ever larger directly ahead. To your left you get a superb view of one of the more fanciful formations in the Park, Three Gossips. There is no trail that leads you closer, but closer would give you a stiff neck and photos so bedeviled with parallax that the Three Gossips would look like three pinheads. Even this view from the Park Avenue trail might be too close, and the photographer might be better served by the view from the Courthouse Towers parking area or the Pipe Organ turnoff.

Near the end, the path goes along a water-pocket fold, a huge stone expanse pock-marked with temporary puddle basins. After crossing a subsidiary wash, the path climbs gradually over sand and eleven easy stairs to the main road.

Many hikers will turn around at the wash and head back the way they came. Another plan is to have a car waiting for you at the Courthouse Towers parking area. But then you forgo the pleasure of the return trip through the canyon and the opportunity to enjoy its beauty from a different perspective. Of course, you also avoid the pleasure of climbing back up the stairs to the parking lot, a pleasure some may be quite willing to give up. But it's a personal choice.

Sheep Rock on the right.

Courthouse Towers near the end of the hike.

Three Gossips.

There is another strategy that avoids the stairs at the Park Avenue Trailhead altogether. Start your hike at the Courthouse Towers parking area, walk to the stairs, turn around, and walk back. But then you miss the excitement of descending into the canyon—again a tradeoff that most will decide to decline.

A waterpocket fold near the end of Park Avenue.

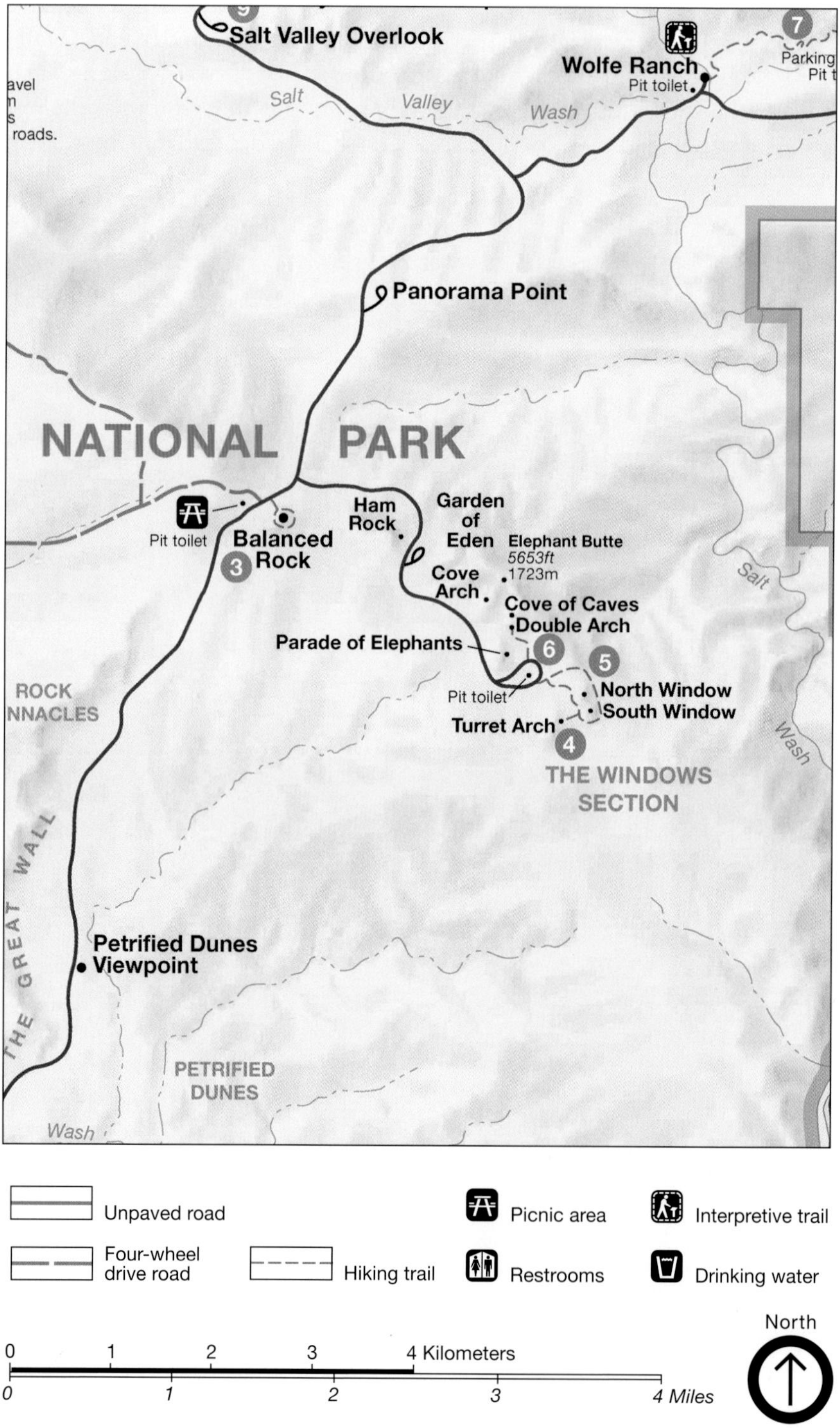

Salt Valley Overlook
Wolfe Ranch
Pit toilet
Parking
7
9
Salt
Valley
Wash
Panorama Point
NATIONAL PARK
Pit toilet
Balanced Rock
3
Ham Rock
Garden of Eden
Elephant Butte
5653ft
1723m
Cove Arch
Cove of Caves
Double Arch
Parade of Elephants
6
5
Pit toilet
North Window
South Window
Turret Arch
4
THE WINDOWS SECTION
Salt
Wash
THE GREAT WALL
Petrified Dunes Viewpoint
PETRIFIED DUNES
Wash
Unpaved road
Four-wheel drive road
Hiking trail
Picnic area
Restrooms
Interpretive trail
Drinking water
0
1
2
3
4 Kilometers
0
1
2
3
4 Miles
North

Balanced Rock — Trail 3

Start:	Balanced Rock parking area, 9 miles from the Visitor Center, on the right.
Distance:	.3 mile (.5 km) round trip.
Elevation gain:	None.
Difficulty:	Easy.

Certainly, one of the more bizarre formations in a national park that boasts many bizarre formations, Balanced Rock is a traffic-stopper—literally, since the structure is in full view from the road. Given the small area it serves, you might think that the parking area is generous. But this is a popular attraction, and it can be filled to capacity at any time of the day. However, it doesn't require much time to walk the trail around this feature, so parking spaces usually open up after a short wait.

The improbable Balanced Rock.

The improbable formation rises to a height of about 100 feet (30 m). The bottom half is a lumpy cone that serves as a pedestal. Perched on top of the pedestal is a massive ellipsoidal boulder balanced on its long axis. Of course, it's not going to topple during your visit, but it's hard to avoid the thought while walking close to the formation. As you stroll the loop trail, grand vistas of the La Sal Mountains open up. There are arches to be seen in the distance, but if you want an impressive shot, a telephoto lens is needed.

In the 1950s, when the Park was still a national monument, a modest house trailer was parked near Balanced Rock. Edward Abbey called it home during those seasons that he was employed as a park ranger. And it was here that he wrote the journals that later became the nucleus of his famous book, *Desert Solitaire*, an autobiographical account of his experiences in desert country. "Abbey's country," he calls it in his book, and his passionate and poetic prose leaves no doubt that it was. Reading his book, seeing this region through his eyes, can only increase your understanding and appreciation of the Park.

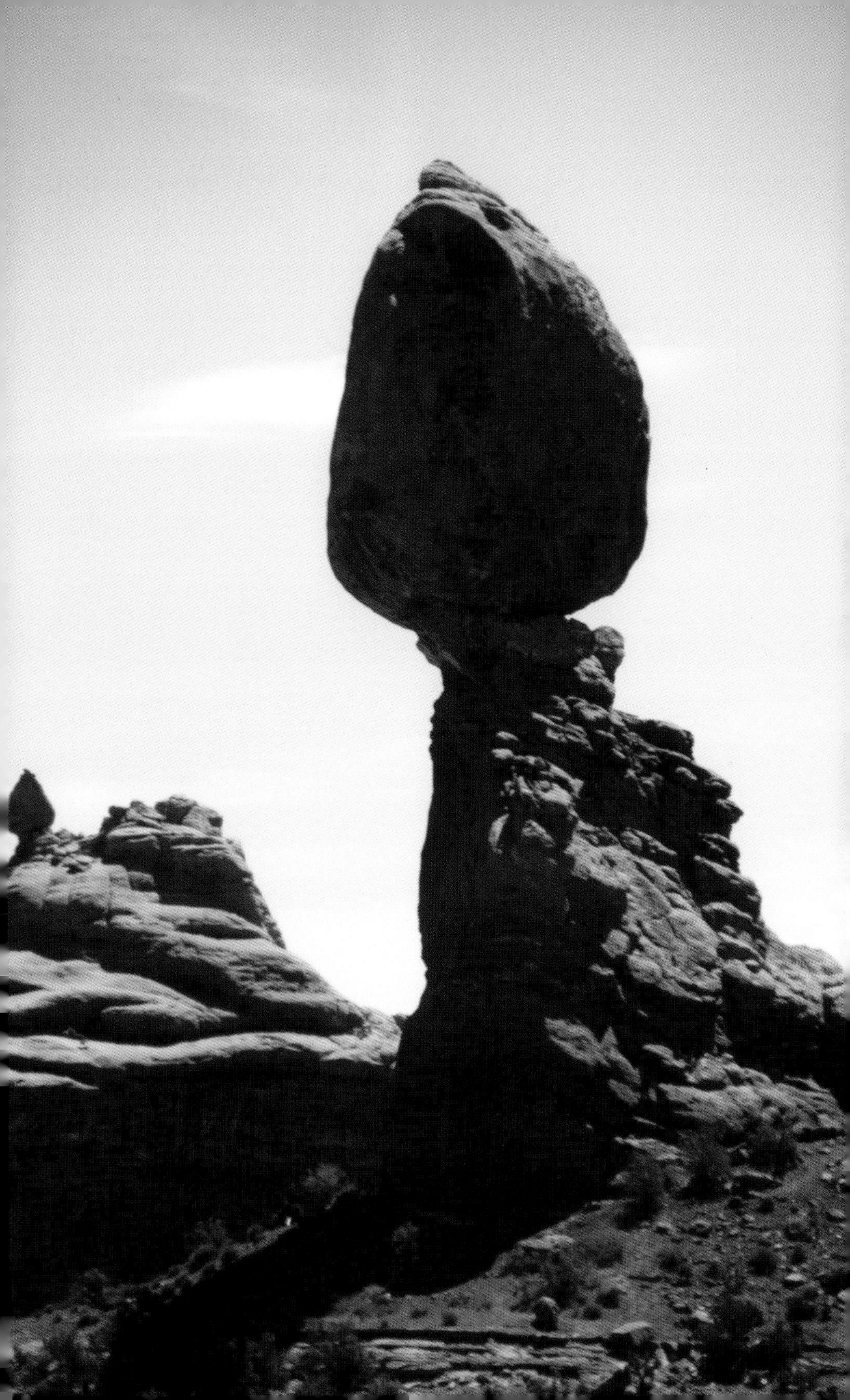

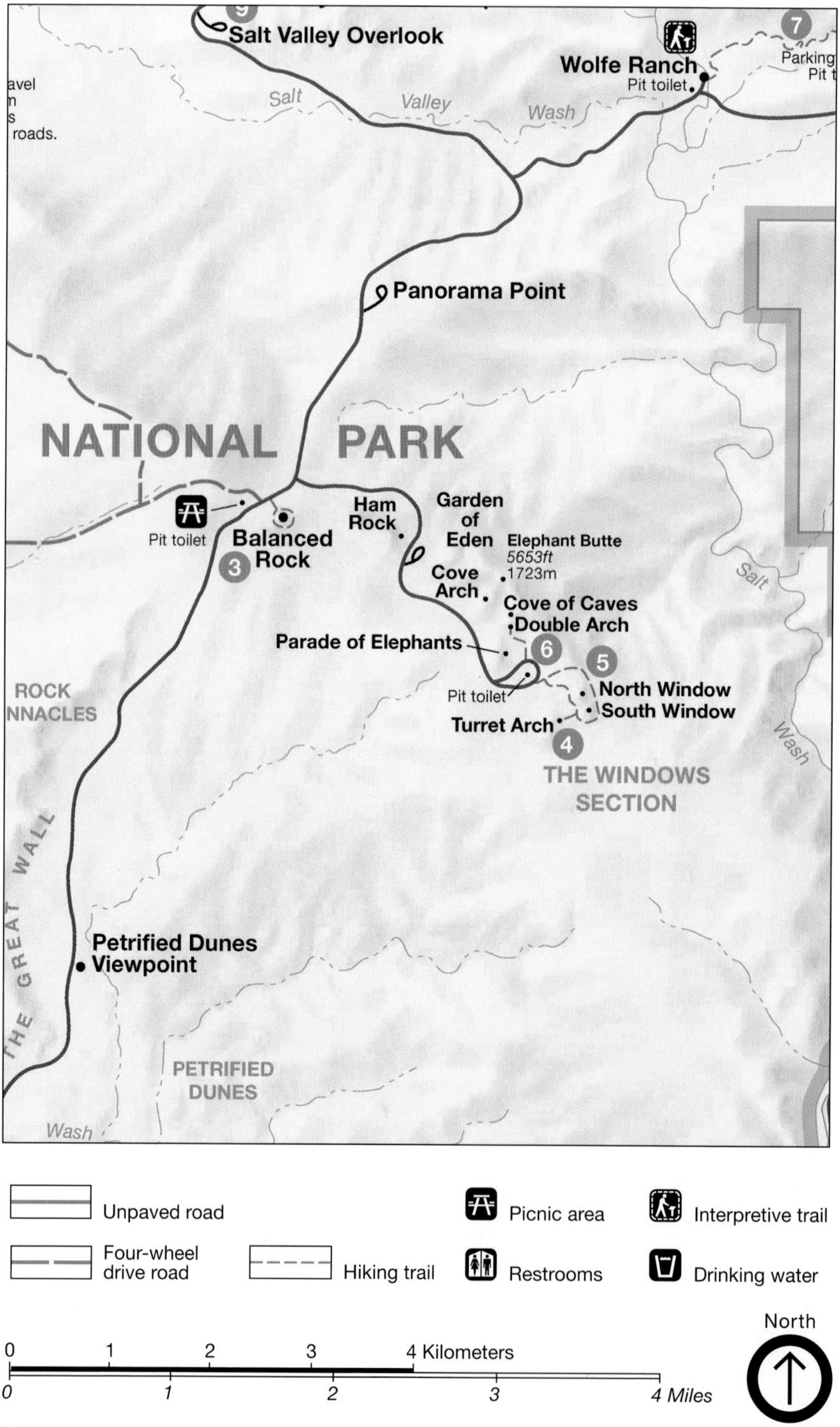

Salt Valley Overlook
9
7
Wolfe Ranch
Pit toilet
Parking
Salt
Valley
Wash
Panorama Point
NATIONAL PARK
Pit toilet
Balanced Rock
3
Ham Rock
Garden of Eden
Elephant Butte
5653ft
1723m
Cove Arch
Cove of Caves
Double Arch
Parade of Elephants
6
5
Pit toilet
North Window
South Window
Turret Arch
4
THE WINDOWS SECTION
Salt
Wash
ROCK
NNACLES
THE GREAT WALL
Petrified Dunes Viewpoint
PETRIFIED DUNES
Wash
Unpaved road
Four-wheel drive road
Hiking trail
Picnic area
Restrooms
Interpretive trail
Drinking water
North
0
1
2
3
4 Kilometers
0
1
2
3
4 Miles

THE WINDOWS SECTION

TRAILS 4 5 6

Start:	The Windows Section parking area, 9.2 miles (14.8 km) from the Visitor Center to a side road on the right, then 2.5 miles (4 km) to the parking circle.
Distance:	.5 mile (.8 km) to The Windows and Turret Arch; .25 mile (.4 km) to Double Arch and Parade of Elephants.
Elevation gain:	Nominal.
Difficulty:	Easy (along main trail) to moderate (along Primitive Trail).

The Windows Section is one of the most popular destinations in Arches National Park, and for good reason. Here you find a concentration of some of the most remarkable features in the Park. Not only are the offerings rich in number, but in variety, as well. Among the main attractions are Turret Arch, Windows, Double Arch, and Parade of Elephants—all within easy walking distance.

The side road to The Windows Section exits east off the main road about 9.2 miles (14.8 km) from the Visitor Center. Then it's a short but scenic drive of 2.5 miles (4 km) to the parking circle where there's ample room, except at peak season when you might have to wait for a space. There are pit toilets adjacent to the parking area but no drinking water.

Alcove and North Window

We begin our tour at the south end of the parking circle, where you find the trailhead to both Turret Arch and Windows. Immediately the trail splits. The left branch becomes the Primitive Trail; the right branch is the main trail. The two trails are roughly the same length, and eventually they join to form a loop. So bearing right or left makes little difference if you intend to do both trails, although the Primitive Trail is somewhat more difficult. We'll start our tour by bearing right onto the main trail.

At the very beginning, off to the left, a large alcove with a prominent cornice is set into a wall of rock. It doesn't take much imagination to see that this is an arch in the making. Sooner or later, in geologic time, the alcove will become deeper and perforate the wall to form a window. Erosion will enlarge the window until it expands to the cornice, creating another grand arch. Throughout this region, particularly near Double Arch, you can see many other examples of the process, showing its different stages.

The trail ascends gradually up a series of stairs, wide enough to accommodate several hikers side-by-side and deep enough, front to back, to require several paces to reach the next step. The steps are made of stone frames surrounding a bed of sand and gravel—not the most natural path, but it serves a large number of visitors without being obtrusive.

Soon North Window comes into view. A side branch of the trail takes you right up to it. Where the trail ends, you can scramble up the rocks to the interior of the arch. It's a great photo op. And if you turn to look west, you get a classic view of Turret Arch, the next big feature on the tour.

Window in the making and North Window—Windows Section.

Stairway to North Window.

Turret Arch

Back on the main trail, it's a short walk to Turret Arch. A stepped spur trail with a bit of steepness takes you up to its base. There, looking back to the east, you get the best simultaneous view of both North and South Windows, positioned side-by-side in a huge wall. With a stretch of the imagination or the help of a bad case of astigmatism, you can see why the formation is sometimes called The Spectacles. The two windows are the lenses, and the massive rock formation between them is the nose.

What Turret Arch lacks in grandeur, it makes up for in whimsy—looking like a child's version of a castle, but boasting only one turret. A very short but steep climb on large blocks of sandstone will take you to the opening and through it to the other side. A stone ramp leads to an interesting but somewhat unstructured formation that has all sorts of potential for climbing and exploring. Even if that's not your game, walk out onto the ramp and see the arch from the west. If you're up to it—in height, that is—

The Windows, sometimes called Spectacles—big nose and all.

Turret Arch—a child's castle.

you can compose a fabulous shot of North Window framed by Turret Arch. When you're ready to return to the main trail, just retrace your steps. Take care coming down. Although most negotiate the descent in proper bipedal fashion, we don't hesitate to use our rumps on the steepest section.

South Window, Raven Roost, and Primitive Trail

Back on the main trail, you continue south, then east, as you round South Window counterclockwise. Just behind the end of South Window, the "improved" main trail ends, and the Primitive Trail begins. Some people choose to return to the parking lot by going back along the main trail. A bit more effort is required to hike back by the Primitive Trail, but it's worth it.

The Primitive Trail begins with a descent to the ground level of a steep-walled concave rampart of stone having extraordinary sound amplification. The upper reaches of this natural auditorium is an aeronautical playground for ravens. Here they perform their high jinks and high-flyer stunt games—

Turret Arch from the west.

aerial-tag, catch-me-if-you-can, come-fly-with-me, and just plain dare—accompanied by boisterous cawing. The raucous ruckus is magnified by the stone structure, acoustics so good that you can clearly hear the flapping of wings. One has to wonder if the birds choose such a haunt, at least in part, because it amplifies the commotion that in turn eggs them on to even greater exploits of derring-do.

After the air show, you can continue back along the Primitive Trail. There are sweeping views off to the east of open desert, punctuated by occasional outcroppings of rock. Close by and to the west, a panoramic view of The Windows unfolds. The trail is well laid out and clearly marked by an edging of stones and occasional cairns. For the most part, it's an easy walk, hardly deserving the term "primitive," but a short stretch within the last quarter of a mile or so justifies the name somewhat.

Most civilized people negotiate this paltry distance—a few paces up, followed by a few down—in a respectable, upright fashion. However, in

Raven roost at south end of The Windows.

accordance with the name of this trail, we choose a more primitive form of locomotion—all fours on the brief ascent, butt-scootch on the steep descent. It's undignified, but it gets us through it safely, albeit a bit red-faced. From here it's a short and easy walk back to the trailhead.

Double Arch and Parade of Elephants

Off the north side of the parking circle is a short trail that takes you to one of the most spectacular arches and one of the most amusing formations in the Park.

Magnificent seen from a distance, Double Arch becomes even more impressive the closer you get to it. But take your time, the approach offers a variety of views, including one of the arch framed by ancient junipers. In season, sand leading to the arch will be studded with bright blue lupines. How strange it is to see these delicate plants on the approach to this massive arch. And the contrast in color—how special and how surprising!

The Windows from the Primitive Trail.

Double Arch.

Bright blue flowers and bright green foliage are set against red sand and a background of red rock.

Double Arch gradually gathers itself up from out of the desert floor in two enormous arcs of stone, in contact at one end, independent at the other. The complexity of this powerful form gives the arch a three-dimensional interest unlike any other. It's pure sculpture.

As you approach the arch, the level trail gives way to stone ledges that provide a route of increasing difficulty up into the heart of the formation. The last few yards are more of a scramble than a walk, but it is far from a technical rock climb. For the effort, you win a high perch with wonderful views. Even a climb part way up will give you a grand view of The Windows and Turret Arch.

Contiguous with Double Arch on the west is a massive, lumpy formation called Parade of Elephants. The name is perfect for this rock-hewn

Double Arch.

pack of pachyderms, but you won't agree if you're too close to the herd. You have to step back fifty feet or so—all the way back to the road is even better—to see the resemblance. At the proper distance, the resemblance is unmistakable, and the lead bull is particularly impressive and convincing.

Heading Back to the Main Road

As you drive back to the main road, take time to visit the Garden of Eden, a large and complex formation of fins. A turnoff with generous parking serves the site, and there are a couple of short walks that will give you a closer look. However, there are no sanctioned trails to the interior of this labyrinth. This is probably a reflection of prudent Park policy. The possibility of getting hopelessly lost in Garden of Eden is not worth the apple. But there is a bit of adventure to be had scrambling among the formations adjacent to the parking area.

While in the parking area for Garden of Eden, take a look at the ham-shaped rock formation—coincidentally called Ham Rock—that is directly

Parade of Elephants.

Garden of Eden—a maze of fins.

Children at play in The Garden of Eden.

Ham Rock.

across the road. It's a curiosity that's certainly worth a glance, but nothing exceptional, given the wonders of The Windows Section.

Another turnoff worth stopping at offers no trails at all. It's a viewpoint for Pot Arch, a feature located high up on a rock formation across the road. If the sun is low in the sky, you'll have to search a bit to find it. The arch opens at a slant, like a bottomless leaning flowerpot, and so is in the shade of its support most of the time. But when the sun is high in the sky, the arch is illuminated and becomes a mysterious glowing orb suspended well above the desert floor.

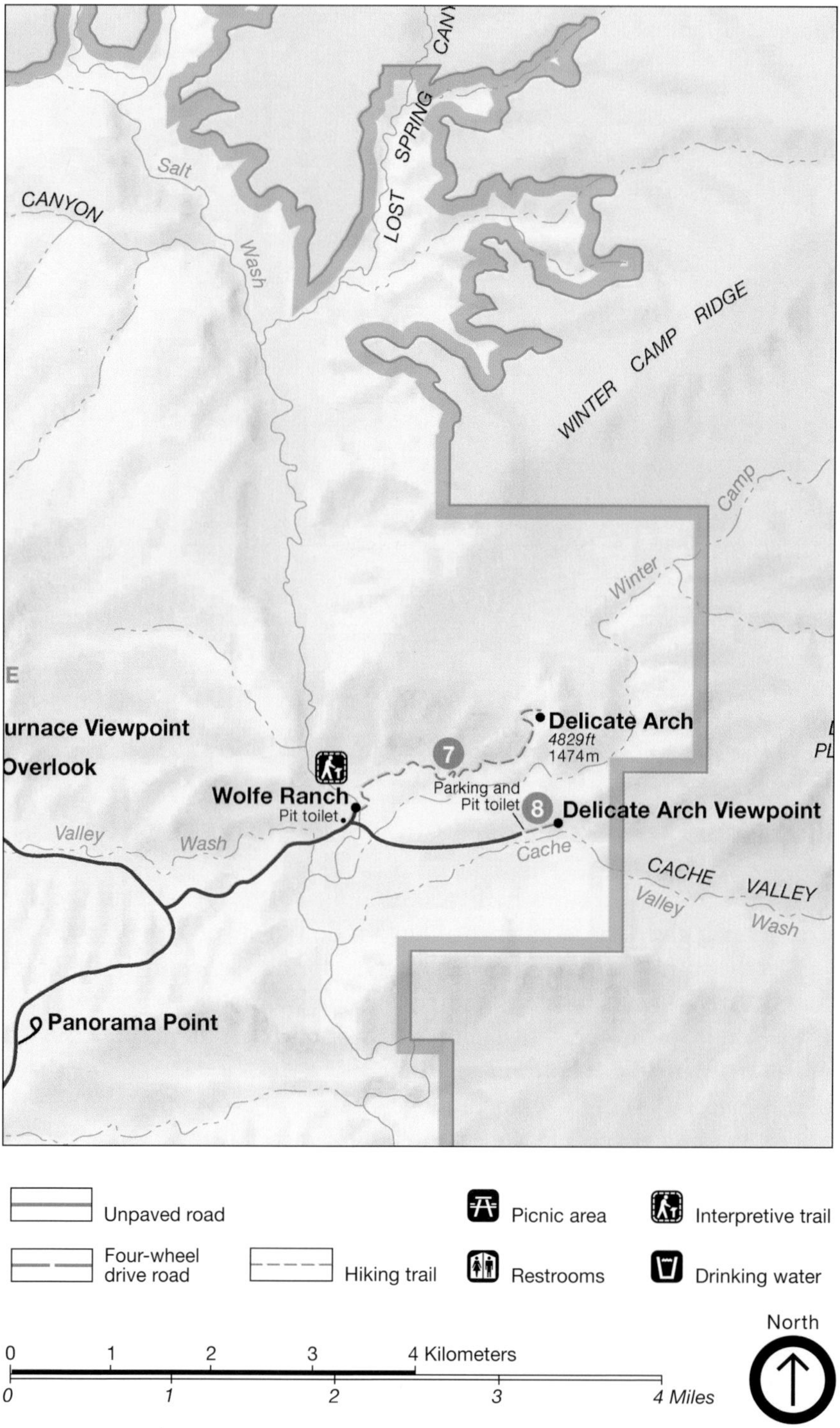

CANYON
Salt
Wash
LOST SPRING CANY
WINTER CAMP RIDGE
Winter
Camp
E
urnace Viewpoint
Overlook
Wolfe Ranch
Pit toilet
Valley
Wash
7
Parking and
Pit toilet
8
Delicate Arch
4829ft
1474m
Delicate Arch Viewpoint
Cache
CACHE VALLEY
Valley
Wash
Panorama Point
PL
Unpaved road
Four-wheel drive road
Hiking trail
Picnic area
Restrooms
Interpretive trail
Drinking water
North
0 1 2 3 4 Kilometers
0 1 2 3 4 Miles

DELICATE ARCH — TRAILS 7 8

Start:	Wolfe Ranch parking area, 11.7 miles (19.9 km) from the Visitor Center to a side road on the right, then 1.2 miles (1.9 km); or Delicate Arch Viewpoint parking area, 1 mile (1.6 km) past the Wolfe Ranch parking area.
Distance:	1.5 miles (2.4 km) round trip; .25 mile (.4 km) from Viewpoint parking area.
Elevation gain:	480 feet (146 m); 100 feet (30 m) from Viewpoint parking area.
Difficulty:	Moderate to moderately strenuous from both parking areas.

Recognized worldwide, Delicate Arch is the emblem of Arches National Park. It's a well-chosen symbol, for there is no feature more distinctive. But its sturdy proportions and Herculean size—over sixty feet (18.3 m) tall—belie its name. Delicate it is not. That moniker is more suited to Landscape Arch than to this one, but call it what you will, this extraordinary formation never fails to evoke awe.

Of course, the setting also adds to the dramatic impact of the scene. The arch, a gigantic horseshoe balanced on its legs, rises in isolation out of a vast sheet of bedrock—an unlikely presence completely dominating the scene. From one viewpoint, along the main trail to Delicate Arch, the La Sal Mountains to the east define the horizon. Another viewpoint, from the south on a side trail, shows the arch perched on the rim of a giant stone basin. The Delicate Arch Viewpoint, reached from a different parking area, shows it in the distance, standing on a long ridge, clearly outlined against the sky.

These three views, so different from one another, are served by different routes, and each route offers memorable scenery along the way. Although it is impossible to grasp the full magnificence of the arch and its surroundings no matter how many times you see it, these three routes will at least give you a start.

Delicate Arch from the Wolfe Ranch Trailhead

The most popular route begins at the Wolfe Ranch parking area. The trailhead is served by a not-too-generous parking lot that is often filled by 10 A.M. during the busiest times of the year. Toilets are available at the perimeter of the lot.

A short walk from the trailhead leads to the Wolfe Ranch. What remains of the ranch is a one-room cabin, a root cellar, and some fences. Arches is a wonderful place to visit, but who would want to live here? Could you live here? John Wesley Wolfe could live here and did, between 1898 and 1910. Water enough for some crops and a few head of cattle came from nearby Salt Wash, although the name suggests otherwise. The original cabin housed John and his son. Later, they replaced it with a larger cabin, the one that you now see, in order to accommodate John's daughter and her family.

A few hundred yards past the cabin, a small swinging bridge takes you across Salt Wash. As is the case with so many watercourses in the Southwest,

Wolfe Ranch—home to the Wolfe family around 1900.

Salt Wash in a strangle hold of tamarisk.

this stream is now being strangled by tamarisk, that unstoppable invader from the Mideast that threatens to establish its hegemony throughout the region. Tamarisk was imported intentionally in the 1920s to control erosion. The unintended consequence of that decision adds one more entry in the long list of examples of tragic environmental tampering.

Just past the bridge, a short side trail branches off to the left and leads to a rock wall. Here you find a Ute rock painting, a petroglyph, showing horsemen hunting or herding various animals. It's not to be missed.

Back on the main trail, a couple of switchbacks leads onto an enormous expanse of rock tilted upward in the general direction of your destination. Now the procession of hikers transforms itself into a joyful pilgrimage. While we are not fond of crowds the general mood along this stretch of trail, in our experience, has always been one of excitement and anticipation, and this has only added to our enjoyment.

So many people have come to see Delicate Arch that a trail has been worn into the solid rock, but the trail is faint and sometimes difficult to see, so watch for the cairns (manmade piles of stones) that mark the way.

Petroglyphs at the end of a side trail near Wolfe Ranch.

Strange as it may seem, you will find a miniature oasis flourishing along the route. Where some excuse for soil has accumulated, in crevices and shallow basins, in places where water can be trapped or has percolated up from underground sources, plants have found a way to take hold and thrive. How wonderful to see these "hanging gardens"! How surprising to see plants usually associated with much posher environments—columbines, ferns, rushes, and even orchids—thriving here! Verdant gardens surrounded by red rock under the desert sun—how unexpected!

These gardens provide no shade, however, and hikers will need protection from the sun; protective clothing and sunscreen are recommended. The trail is steep enough and hot enough to dehydrate you quickly, so take plenty of water.

The trek across the rock accounts for most of the distance to the arch, but after almost 1.5 miles (2.4 km), the trail finally funnels onto a rock ledge about 200 yards (183 m) long. The traverse slices along a wall rising to your right and falling twenty feet (6.1 m) or so on your left. The path is wide enough to accommodate two abreast, but in some places, barely so.

In places the drop is steep enough and deep enough to warrant some caution. Beware of running children. Even those a bit tired by the trek across the rock slab are fully energized on the traverse, and they love to dash along its length from either direction toward the other. Nevertheless, few hikers will find that these high jinks or the exposure will cause them much concern.

Along the traverse, there is no sign of the arch. At the very end, it appears suddenly, dramatically, and in full view. There, on a balcony, you will likely find a crowd, transfixed in amazement, like fans in a stadium watching a great sporting event. The celebratory atmosphere is infectious, and you will probably not mind the company at all.

A level line of sight focuses your gaze a third of the way up from the base, but the whole arch is there in front of you, as well as the La Sal Mountains on the horizon and the enormous stone platform that supports the arch.

There is no more wondrous or spectacular view in the Park. But as spectacular as this view is, few will remain standing on the balcony for long. The temptation to get up close to the arch is irresistible. A low wall separates you from the arch, but there are several places where you can easily and safely climb over the wall and go right up to the arch. It's an unforgettable experience.

True, this hike is unbeatable, but there are two others that will give you a different perspective and add a great deal more to your appreciation of this singular landmark.

Delicate Arch—the Park's icon.

Delicate Arch View from Wolfe Ranch Trailhead, Alternate Route

A second route starts from the same trailhead and proceeds as the one just described until you are within fifty yards (46 m) or so of the final traverse. Here, the alternate route branches off to the right and is none-too-clearly marked. You climb a low wall and swing left proceeding uphill. A larger step of rock will require a helping hand or a less-dignified method to scale. A quadrupedal maneuver works quite well. A short walk takes you to the outer reaches of a vast stone bowl.

There, directly across the bowl, on its far rim, you see Delicate Arch. The people swarming at its base seem to be the size of ants, so great is the distance. You can wander at will around the sides of the bowl and play hide-and-seek among the rock formations on your side of the rim. But the sides of the bowl are so steep that an attempt to descend into it and reach the arch would be foolhardy. The bowl is a fascinating and puzzling feature in its own right, and we have no idea of how it was formed. Of course, there on its far side, is its unique handle, Delicate Arch.

Delicate Arch sits on the rim of a giant sandstone bowl.

Delicate Arch Viewpoint

Another trail that deserves exploring takes you to Delicate Arch Viewpoint. Parking at this trailhead, one mile (1.6 km) past the Wolfe Ranch parking area, is limited, but this route draws fewer people. Nevertheless, it offers its own attractions and is well worth visiting.

Within 100 yards (91 m) of the parking area, there is a wheelchair accessible viewpoint. However, the trail beyond it takes you closer and gives you a far more scenic viewing platform.

From the trailhead, it's a short but moderately steep walk up to a plateau that provides an excellent view, no matter where you stand. There to the north, across a steep ravine preventing closer access, you see the arch. How strange to see it in isolation, set against the sky, atop a long ridge of rock, and the focus of a gawking swarm of visitors milling around its base like ants. Marvelous as it appears to the naked eye, some will rely on binoculars or a telephoto lens to provide a closer look.

Delicate Arch from the end of Delicate Arch Viewpoint Trail.

Fewer people and more room per person gives this viewpoint less of a carnival atmosphere. It's a more relaxing site and a perfect place to contemplate the wonders of the region.

You will want to spend some time exploring the plateau itself. There are interesting views to be had in almost all directions, and the plateau is not at all barren. Dwarfed and twisted junipers illustrate the tenacity needed to survive in this sun-baked, wind-battered region. On the other hand, the many wildflowers hunkering close to the ground or against boulders have a fragile appearance that seems to contradict their situation.

The trail offers another feature that some will find strangely beautiful, while others will see it as just plain ugly. To the east of the trail is a hillside of bright blue. Its appearance is perfectly poisonous, and most who see it guess that it's slag tossed down from some man-inflicted mining wound. No such thing. It's merely copper that has worked its way to the surface naturally. Beautiful or ugly may be a personal call in this case, but it is undeniably interesting.

Copper from a natural deposit colors the hillside blue.

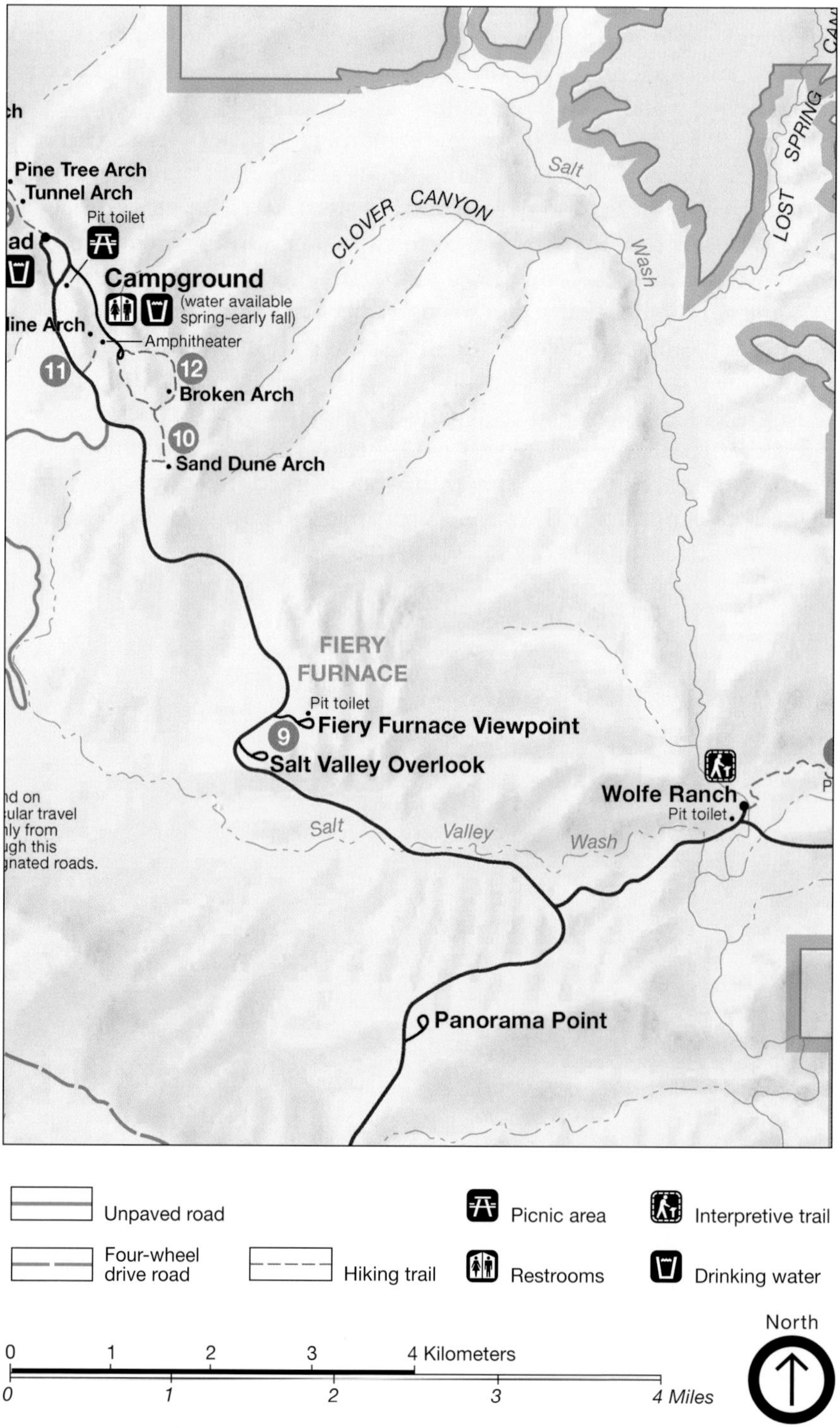

ch
Pine Tree Arch
Tunnel Arch
Pit toilet
ad
Campground
(water available spring-early fall)
line Arch
Amphitheater
11
12
Broken Arch
10
Sand Dune Arch
CLOVER CANYON
Salt
Wash
LOST SPRING
FIERY FURNACE
Pit toilet
Fiery Furnace Viewpoint
9
Salt Valley Overlook
Wolfe Ranch
Pit toilet
Salt Valley Wash
Panorama Point
nd on
ular travel
nly from
gh this
gnated roads.
Unpaved road
Four-wheel drive road
Hiking trail
Picnic area
Restrooms
Interpretive trail
Drinking water
North
0 1 2 3 4 Kilometers
0 1 2 3 4 Miles

Fiery Furnace — Trail 9

Start: Fiery Furnace parking area, 14.5 miles (23.3 km) from the Visitor Center, to the right, off the main road.
Distance: 2 miles (3.2 km).
Elevation gain: About 150 feet (45 m), but with several short stretches of scrambling up or down over rock.
Difficulty: Moderately strenuous.

If it's adventure you're looking for—a hike filled with wonder and excitement—you can do no better than sign up for a tour of Fiery Furnace. It's a journey into a surreal landscape, a labyrinth of narrow corridors connecting hidden grottos and secluded chambers filled with fantastic forms: pillars, slot canyons, hidden alcoves, and fanciful arches. Just maneuvering through the maze is an adventure. There are ledges to traverse, passages to step through, and crevices to straddle. Each step, each turn, brings new surprises.

All of this is crammed into a hike of only two miles (3.2 km). The hike takes three hours, hardly enough time to do it justice. This is a tour that trumps imagination. It's one to remember.

Entrance into Fiery Furnace is by permit only. Ranger-guided tours are given twice daily between April and October. The cost is currently $8 for adults and $4 for children six to twelve years old and Golden Age Passport holders. Permits must be purchased in person at the Visitor Center and are offered on a first-come, first-served basis. The number of people allowed on each tour is limited. Since these very popular hikes may be filled days in advance, it's important to sign up early.

You can also get a permit to do it alone, but keep in mind that you'll be entering a confusing labyrinth with no trails, no cairns, and no directional signs. Since much of the hike is through washes and over slickrock, you cannot depend on following the footprints of others, and it's all too easy to get lost. So, unless you've had considerable experience in this complex maze, a ranger-led tour is your safest and best bet.

A few preparations will ensure that it's a safe and enjoyable tour. Each person should carry at least one quart (about one liter) of water. Footwear with adequate traction is advised. Hiking poles are more of a hindrance than a convenience, since the hike requires the use of both hands in order to maneuver through narrow cracks and to grasp handholds in the rock while moving along ledges. If you bring along a camera, carry it in a case that will protect it from hitting the rock walls.

The physical demands of the hike include: scrambling over boulders and onto ledges; walking on narrow fins (but always with a wall on one side); climbing through short, narrow chutes (usually on rock stairs); maneuvering through narrow slots; sidling through wedges; staying upright on somewhat inclined ledges; and braving moderate exposure.

So with permit in hand and all preparations in place, you head off to the parking area that serves both the Fiery Furnace trailhead and a viewpoint. The viewpoint is reached by a walkway that leaves the parking loop and heads east for a few hundred feet. In the distance you see the La Sal Mountains dominating the horizon. Much closer and to the north is the complex of fins that form Fiery Furnace. From here you only see the exterior of the maze. It's an impressive sight, but it gives no hint as to what you find inside.

A fence borders the entire parking loop and viewpoint trail. There is a pit toilet (remember, it's a three-hour hike), but no drinking water. The one gate marks the trailhead and carries a sign saying that entrance is by permit only. Since the hikes start on time, you may want to arrive fifteen minutes or so beforehand to allow yourself time to get organized.

At the designated time, the ranger arrives and gathers her flock by the gate. She makes some introductory remarks, issues some warnings, and answers questions. Then the adventure begins.

At first it's gradually downhill and in the open. The group stops at a stone outcropping, and the ranger tells them more about the area. Then again she gathers her flock together, and the group descends into a wash (the bed of a temporary stream). Even without rain for weeks, the sand in the wash is moist below the surface. You can even find small pools choked with algae. You can also find poison ivy ("leaves of three, let it be") thriving in the moist sand and in the shade of rocks.

A few more steps and the group enters the confines of Fiery Furnace. Suddenly you're in a narrow passageway with walls towering above you. Instantly it's cooler and much shadier, with only isolated patches of sky to be seen and occasional splashes of sunshine on the rocks. The group has breached some ancient fortress, and conversation is excited, but muted and respectful.

Soon you come to what looks like a more traditional entrance—no matter that you are already inside. It's an arch that connects the side walls

The adventure begins—walking down to the Fiery Furnace.

of the passageway. This is Walk Through Arch, and that's what you do. You walk through it and continue.

A bit farther on, the ranger points out a small opening straddling a sluiceway about eight feet (3 m) above. It's Crawl Through Arch, and it barely passes the test for being an arch. (To do so, an opening must be large enough to accommodate a yardstick oriented in any direction about some point.) Those dressed for the occasion will scramble up and crawl through Crawl Through Arch just for the bragging rights, if nothing else, although it's not that difficult.

The hike continues by twists and turns: short traverses along ledges, maneuvers through slots, and scrambles up on rocks and through passageways connecting grottos, small amphitheaters, and secret sanctuaries. All around are strange and fascinating forms—modern abstract sculpture, primitive icons, and a gallery of improbable creations showing Nature's more whimsical side. In the words of Lewis Carroll, "Curiouser and curiouser."

Walk Through Arch.

Crawl Through Arch.

The odyssey continues through the narrow passages of the maze, until suddenly you find yourself in a large grotto. Raven Canyon, it's called, since it's a favorite haunt of those black harbingers of gloom. But what really gives the chamber its sepulchral aura is the large double arch that dominates the upper reaches, the macabre Skull Arch, a death's head framed against the sky, with great vacant eyes staring down at you. Transfixed, the group stares back. Some shake their heads in disbelief, some in amazement. A few chuckle with just a hint of nervousness. Finally, freeing themselves of the spectral gaze of Skull Arch, the group moves on.

The ranger leads the group from corridor to corridor and finally onto a wide ledge. A wall joins the ledge in back of the group and rises above them. It's a perfect impromptu amphitheater. When the group is seated, the ranger moves to the very edge of the ledge, unconcerned about the drop behind her, the most significant exposure on the hike.

The ranger explains that in the darkness behind the group, where the ceiling meets the floor, there are gaps large enough to accommodate the middens (nests) of pack rats. These creatures gather seeds and other foodstuffs and store them back there. They also scavenge bones, car keys, coins, rings, and other treasures and store this booty as well—for fun or profit, no

Skull Arch.

one knows. But some scientists have studied these middens (someone's got to do it) and have carbon-dated them back some 40,000 years, providing insight into the geological and biological history of the region. Don't expect to see the pack rats—they're nocturnal.

Again, the hike gets under way, and again the intricacies of the labyrinth have your attention. You cannot help but wonder what you would do if suddenly you found yourself alone. However, you're in a group, and the ranger knows the way. Soon she leads you into another chamber, The Garden, and any gloominess that might have followed you out of Raven Canyon and persisted through the discussion of pack rats now vanishes.

The Garden looks like ... a garden. Not a regimented formal garden in the French style, nor an exuberant formless garden in the English cottage style. This landscape has the restraint and refinement of a Japanese garden. Even the plants are reserved, but each is given its due. Rocks provide contrast and structure. Sand is the ground cover.

The Garden would seem to be the perfect spot for a serious moment, a moment of quiet meditation. That is until you notice Kissing Turtles Arch. There they are, perched on a shelf of rock protruding from a wall, two stone turtles standing on their hind whatevers joined at the lips in a smootch for

Cartoon in stone—Kissing Turtles Arch.

the ages. Hilarious, although it totally destroys the contemplative aspect of the chamber. Never mind—it's wonderful.

The group leaves The Garden and continues through the maze. Some are still chuckling and talking about Kissing Turtles when they enter another chamber. There, high above, outlined against the sky, is Surprise Arch. According to the ranger, this was not its original name. As the story goes, Superintendent Bates Wilson was exploring this section of Fiery Furnace in December of 1963. Hail had started to fall, and the slickrock became, well, slick. Bates slipped and fell. He picked himself up and simultaneously glanced up. There was the arch. "Son-of-a-bitch," he exclaimed, succinctly expressing both his displeasure at falling and the pleasure of discovering the arch. And so Son-of-a-bitch Arch it became for those in the know. But ever mindful of the general public's genteel sensibilities, it was renamed Surprise Arch.

Surprise Arch (aka SOB Arch).

It's a quick three hours, and Surprise Arch is the last highlight of this magical journey. On one tour, ranger-guide Miriam Graham treated the group to a flute solo; then she quoted a passage from Edward Abbey's *Desert Solitaire*. Perfect!

Leaving Surprise Arch, you climb down a narrow crack along a fin, then up a bit, and then out between two fins and into the open. From here it's a short walk back to the parking lot.

If your tour ends in late afternoon, look back to where you were only a few minutes earlier. There you will see rock formations in deep shadow, cradling a cluster of fins and pinnacles painted orange-red by the sun—like flames leaping from a cauldron of coals. Fiery Furnace.

Fiery Furnace indeed.

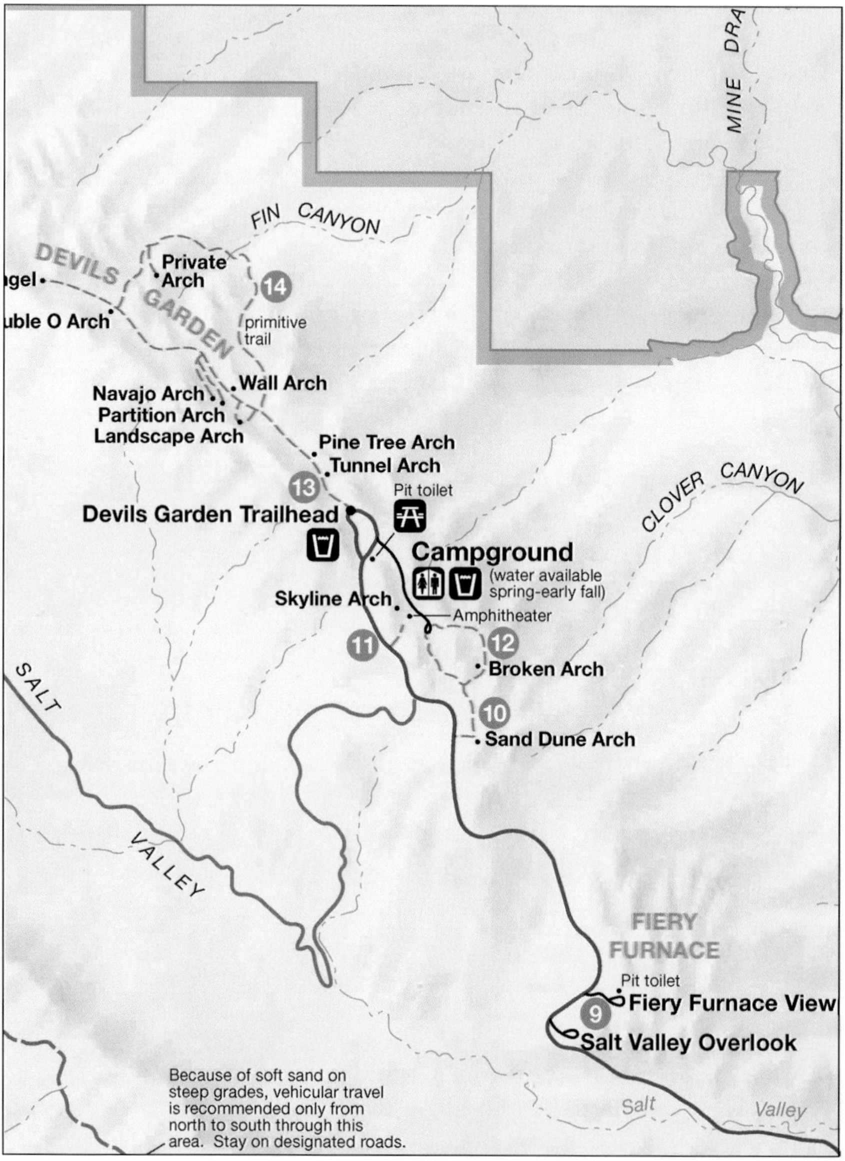

Unpaved road

Four-wheel drive road

Hiking trail

Picnic area

Restrooms

Interpretive trail

Drinking water

0 1 2 3 4 Kilometers

0 1 2 3 4 Miles

North

Broken Arch and Sand Dune Arch Trails 10 12

Start:	Sand Dune Arch parking area, 17 miles (27.4 km) from the Visitor Center on the right.
Distance:	.6 mile (1 km) to Broken Arch; .2 mile (.3 km) to Sand Dune Arch.
Elevation gain:	Negligible.
Difficulty:	Easy.

Starting from a shared trailhead, very little effort will get you to two distinctly different arches—one bold and exposed, the other more delicate and hidden from view. The walk to each is special in its own way.

Broken Arch

This is an easy walk, almost all of it on sand across open desert. What makes it so rewarding? It's a high-contrast study in color, form, and texture—red sand, blue-gray sage, a background of red rock, and on most days, a bluer than blue sky.

A short distance from the trailhead, the trail splits, with the left fork leading toward a wall of stone and Broken Arch. As you approach, you get a glimpse of Broken Arch set somewhat back of the wall and partly hidden by it. Near the wall, the trail turns to the right and becomes more stony and uneven, but it never really presents a challenge. Soon you reach the arch. It's large. It's massive. It's grand. The fine, transverse crack at its apex gives the arch its name but barely suggests the weakness in its sturdy form that will eventually lead to its collapse. You can go up to it (through it, if you want) and continue on the trail to the Devils Garden Campground.

Getting up to the opening requires a bit of a scramble. The hiker has to climb onto a sloping ledge by scaling its vertical, chest-high face. A makeshift stack of stones and the trunk of a dead juniper serve as a staircase. This helps, but it's still a scramble. However, many do it, including children and others whose enthusiasm trumps caution.

On the way to Broken Arch.

Sand Dune Arch

Here's a trail for children and for the child in all of us. It's short on effort, but long on variety and surprises.

Soon after leaving the trailhead that serves both Broken Arch and Sand Dune Arch, the trail splits. The right fork leads to Sand Dune Arch, but first directly toward a close-packed formation of fins. A dead-end? Not at all. As you approach, you discover a gap between two of the fins

Improbable as it first seems, the trail continues with a bit of scrambling, up through the gap to a sandy landing surrounded by stone walls. At first, the arch is hidden. But take a few more steps, and suddenly it appears in an alcove to your right. It's a large and massive arch with a prominent fissure

Broken Arch.

at the top, more suggestive of a broken arch than Broken Arch. There's a wall close behind the arch, but the arch stands clear of it, and you can walk through it to the wall.

Within the grotto that houses the arch, there are two very short spur trails that narrow to nothing in a few paces. You can climb onto a ledge that borders one of them and enthrone yourself as ruler of this tiny domain, at least ruler for the moment. The coronation provides a great photo op.

The entire hidden chamber, with its improbable arch, seems the perfect place for some mystical rite of a long-gone culture. The whole scene would be seriously mysterious, were it not for the prevailing sense of playfulness.

The colony of fins that houses Sand Dune Arch.

The passageway to Sand Dune Arch.

Sand Dune Arch in its hidden chamber.

Sand Dune Arch from the back wall.

Passages in the Sand Dune Arch chamber.

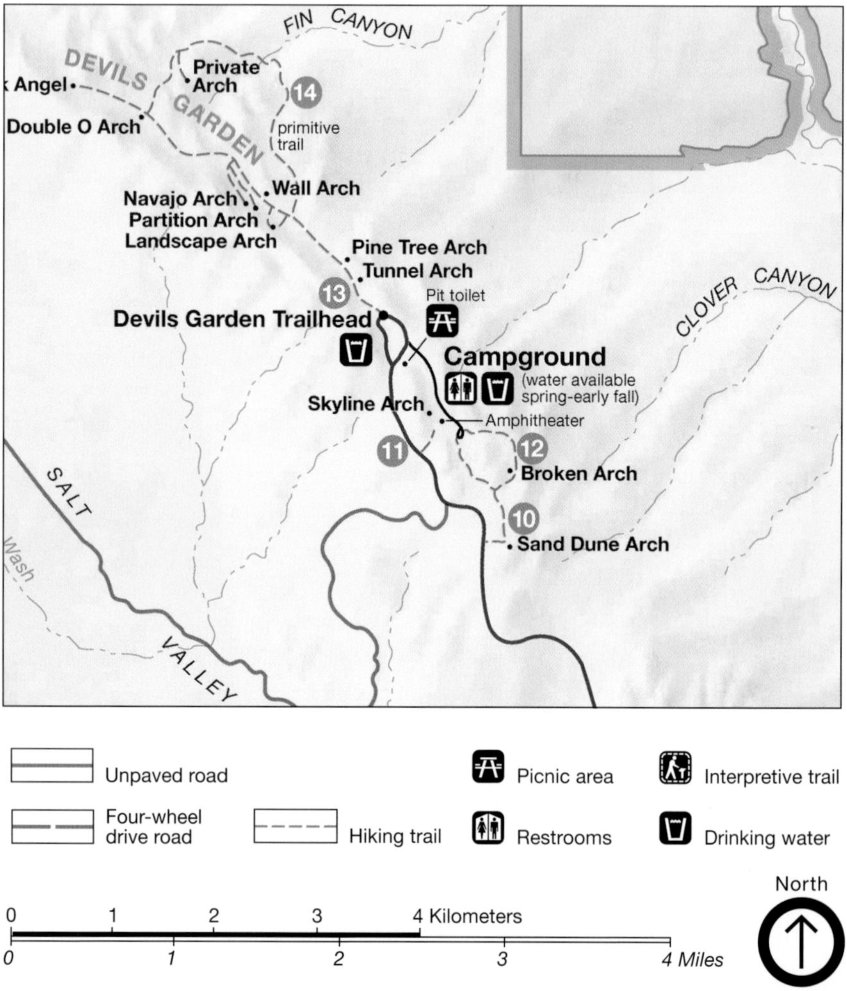
FIN CANYON
DEVILS GARDEN
Angel
Private Arch
14
Double O Arch
primitive trail
Wall Arch
Navajo Arch
Partition Arch
Landscape Arch
Pine Tree Arch
Tunnel Arch
13
Pit toilet
Devils Garden Trailhead
CLOVER CANYON
Campground
(water available spring-early fall)
Skyline Arch
Amphitheater
11
12
Broken Arch
10
Sand Dune Arch
SALT VALLEY
Wash
Unpaved road
Four-wheel drive road
Hiking trail
Picnic area
Restrooms
Interpretive trail
Drinking water
0 1 2 3 4 Kilometers
0 1 2 3 4 Miles
North

Skyline Arch

Trail 11

Start:	Skyline Arch parking area, a turnoff about 18.5 miles (29.8 km) from the Visitor Center, on the right.
Distance:	.2 mile (.3 km) round trip.
Elevation gain:	Negligible.
Difficulty:	Easy.

This is an imposing arch, large and powerfully formed. You can see it from the main road; you can see it from anywhere along the road to Klondike Bluffs. And from wherever you see it, it's a prominent feature of the skyline, hence its name.

The opening is so high above the desert floor that no earthbound objects are visible through it, so the arch is a window to the sky—pure sky with no clutter. It's always impressive, but never more so than when the rock glows red in the late afternoon sun and the sky is a cloudless deep blue.

Geologic change, the kind that sculpts arches, is usually thought to proceed slowly in geologic time, but occasionally change is sudden and dramatic, as was the case sometime in November of 1940. With no one around to see it or hear it, a huge mass of rock broke free of the arch and fell to the base of the fin. In that instant, Skyline Arch doubled the size of its opening.

Skyline Arch punctuates the rock rampart, as seen from the Klondike Bluffs road.

Skyline Arch.

The trail begins at the perimeter of a turnoff along the main road. Parking is limited, and during peak season, you may have to wait for a space. The trail is short and easy. Too bad, because a prize like this deserves more effort. Although the approach is direct and you never lose sight of the arch, the view changes. At first you see the arch framed in the gap between two fins. As the path takes you through the gap, the arch and the desert floor leading up to it fills your view—red sand, pale blue-gray sage, red arch, blue sky. Have your camera ready!

At the base of the arch is that heap of stone that fell from it in 1940. You can climb up onto the heap, but the arch is so immense that there is not much change in perspective. Climbing up into the opening itself seems impossible; the wall is vertical and the opening is far above the ground. But if you look closely at the photo on page 83, you will see some poet-scholar perched inside the arch, engrossed in a book. How did he get there? We have no idea.

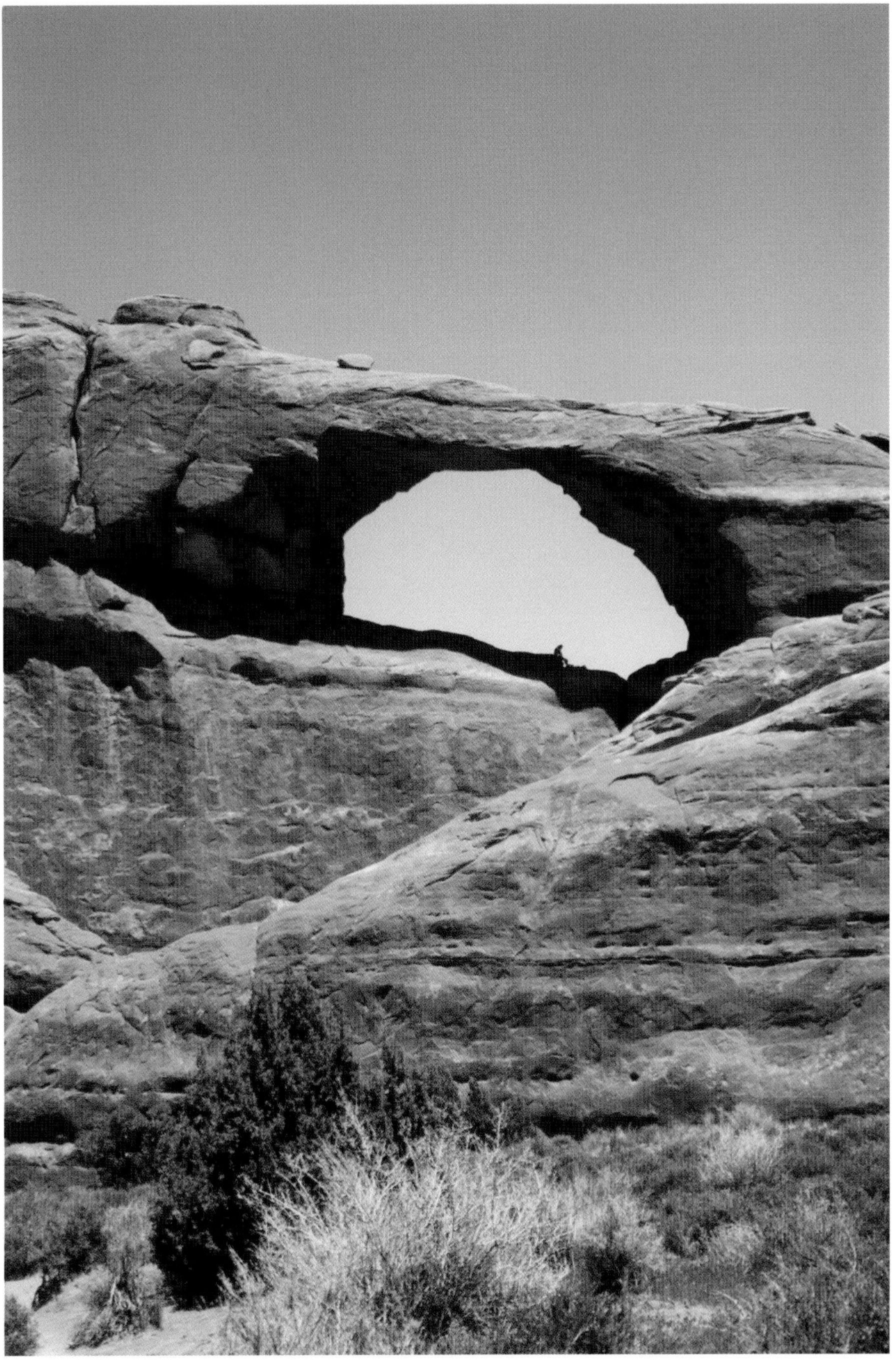

Skyline Arch—can you see the person inside the arch?

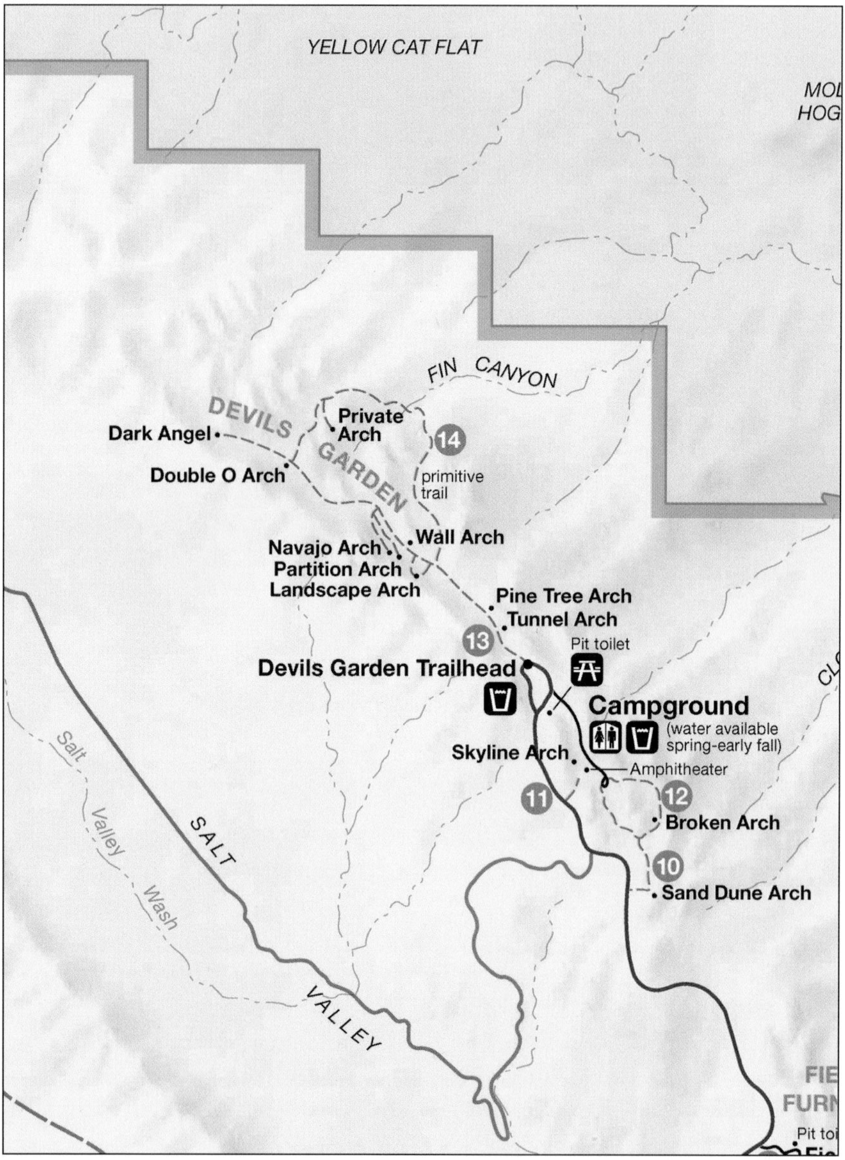

YELLOW CAT FLAT
MOL
HOG
FIN CANYON
DEVILS GARDEN
Private Arch
14
primitive trail
Dark Angel
Double O Arch
Wall Arch
Navajo Arch
Partition Arch
Landscape Arch
Pine Tree Arch
Tunnel Arch
13
Pit toilet
Devils Garden Trailhead
Campground
(water available spring-early fall)
Skyline Arch
Amphitheater
11
12
Broken Arch
10
Sand Dune Arch
Salt Valley Wash
SALT VALLEY
FIE
FURN
Pit toi

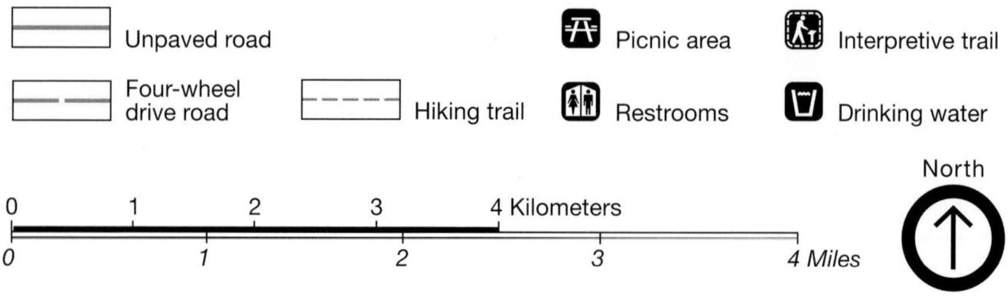

Unpaved road
Four-wheel drive road
Hiking trail
Picnic area
Restrooms
Interpretive trail
Drinking water
North
0
1
2
3
4 Kilometers
0
1
2
3
4 Miles

The Devils Garden Region

Trails 13 14

Start:	Devils Garden parking area, at the end of the main road, 19 miles (31 km) from the Visitor Center.	
Distance one-way in miles (kilometers):		
	Tunnel Arch	.4 (.6)
	Pine Tree Arch	.4 (.6)
	Landscape Arch	.8 (1.3)
	Wall Arch	1 (1.6)
	Partition Arch	1.4 (2.2)
	Navajo Arch	1.5 (2.4)
	Double O Arch	2 (3.2)
	Dark Angel	2.5 (4)
	Private Arch	2.9 (4.6)
Elevation gain:	Nominal to Landscape Arch, steep for the next .2 mi (.3 km), and mostly level stretches farther on.	
Difficulty:	Easy to strenuous, depending on your choice of destination.	

At the end of the main road is the region called Devils Garden. Far from being hellish, this garden is a grand gallery of freeform sculpture, the work of Nature at her mind-boggling best. Of course, there are arches, a rich assortment of arches. This is the realm of Landscape Arch, recognized as the world's longest free span of stone. And there are fins, the best examples to be found anywhere. Added to these attractions are windows and alcoves, arches in the making, as well as towers, columns, spires, and pinnacles. It all combines to make a hike as varied and rewarding as any in the Park.

Even if you were to walk the trails without ever looking up, there would be pleasure in that. Some sections are smooth and broad. A few are narrow, steep, and rocky. Some places even offer a bit of exposure (avoidable if you wish). But you can easily customize the hike to suit your abilities and goals by turning back whenever you wish. For most hikers, that point will be at the very end of the trail.

The trailhead is on the perimeter of the parking lot. Nearby are pit toilets and a drinking fountain. There are no other facilities along the hike. No sooner do you start the hike, than something special comes into view. To your left, captured between two walls of stone, is a strongly inclined sand chute. Children love it, and those off leash never tire of playing king-of-the-mountain on the slope. Cryptobiotic soil is nowhere to be found.

Tunnel Arch

After .3 mile (.5 km), a side trail exits on the right and soon forks. The right-hand branch leads to Tunnel Arch, a short distance away. The arch is impressive, large and powerfully formed. The opening is high up and the rock is smooth, so it's not clear how you would climb into it. We have never seen anyone inside the arch. Another opening, a window too small to be classified as an arch, adds to the interest, and the entire structure suggests the front of an ancient building.

Pine Tree Arch

Back to the fork in the side trail, the left branch soon brings you to Pine Tree Arch. This is a large structure, supported by a pillar on one side and joined to a fin on the other, a sort of flying buttress. The arch gets its name from the large pine tree growing next to it. It's a nice distinguishing feature, but hopefully the arch will outlast it by a long, long time.

The arch frames a striking view of a valley of fins, those great stone walls aligned in parallel, like a regatta of sailing ships passing the review stands. To get an unframed view of the fleet and a different perspective of the arch, you need only walk through it.

For a photo op of people leaning against the free leg of the arch, you may have to exercise some patience and wait your turn.

Landscape Arch

A mere .4 mi (.6 km) farther is Landscape Arch. One of the most renowned features in the Park, Landscape Arch lays claim to being the longest natural span in the world. It's a titanic taffy-pull of stone, stretching some 306 feet (over 93 m) from one end to the other. It's so thin, that one would be tempted to name it Delicate Arch, but that name is already taken.

Clearly, this structurally infeasible feature will not last forever. In fact, in 1991 a sixty-foot (18-m) slab broke loose from the underside of the arch and cracked into a heap of boulders, blocking the path that gavc visitors a chance to get right next to the arch. That path is still closed.

Sand chute, just for children.

Tunnel Arch.

Pine Tree Arch.

Pine Tree Arch extends one leg from a fin.

A grand fin seen from Pine Tree Arch.

Landscape Arch, the longest free span of stone in the world.

Landscape Arch is visible from the approach long before you get there and also from additional viewpoints along the trail as it continues past. Yet, the enormous extent of the arch and the flatness of its arc make composing a photo something of a challenge. But there's nothing else like it, and surely, if you have a camera, you have to try.

If your camera has a telephoto lens or you're armed with binoculars, look up and to the right. What appears to be a small opening is really a good-sized arch. It's Partition Arch, and it's definitely on our itinerary. The hike will take us to the other side and within touching distance.

Partition Arch, seen from Landscape Arch through a telephoto lens.

After leaving Landscape Arch, the trail becomes steeper and rockier. Occasionally the path incorporates boulders as stairs. Now the route is harder to discern, but it has been marked by cairns, those piles of rocks used as guideposts. The cairns have been placed close enough to each other so that as you leave one, you will see the next. In only .2 mile (.3 km) you will meet another arch. This one is to the right of the trail and at a higher level.

Wall Arch

Wall Arch frames a wall of rock. If you go through the arch, a series of ledges will allow you to scramble part way up the wall. You may not get a better view from up there, and some unappreciative photographers might find that your presence does nothing for the composition of the scene.

Wall Arch.

Pause awhile to look at the fin housing the arch. The stone has been carved into an abstract bas-relief. It's quite beautiful, but even finer examples will be found up ahead.

After leaving Wall Arch, the main trail continues in a steep and rocky ascent. But soon it levels out, and the hike becomes a stroll once again as it reaches the side trail that leads to Navajo and Partition arches.

Navajo Arch

Within a few hundred yards, the side trail forks. The right branch goes to Navajo Arch, .4 mile (.6 km) from Wall Arch; the left goes to Partition Arch, .5 mile (.8 km) from Wall Arch. Along the way to either arch, you'll find some of the finest examples of naturally engraved rock in the Park—wonderfully abstract patterns in bas-relief, carved out by the elements. Adding painting to sculpture, other parts of the walls are patterned with lichens and mineral stains.

Cliff Rose and etched stone on the way to Navajo Arch and Partition Arch.

Mineral stain paints an abstract pattern on rock on the path to Navajo Arch and Partition Arch.

An oak growing on sand.

Looking out from Navajo Arch.

Vestibule at Navajo Arch.

You will also find several interesting varieties of plants, some growing out of rock seams, others right out of the sand. Other plants bloom profusely in their season, in seeming contradiction to the surroundings.

Navajo Arch is one of the most hospitable in the park. It's not very large, but it is beautifully sited. Its vestibule is a lovely xeriscape garden, complete with a stone bench surrounded by a mixture of trees and shrubs. It's a wonderful place to enjoy a snack and a bit of rest.

This is not the only amenity that the arch offers. Its supporting structure has a shallow cave—an alcove, you can call it—where the visitor can find welcomed shade while enjoying the view out into the garden.

You will want to spend some time here. When you're ready to leave, simply backtrack to the fork and take the other branch to Partition Arch.

Partition Arch

The walk from the fork to Partition Arch is about the same length as that to Navajo Arch, and it's just as rich in scenery. The arch gets its name from

Partition Arch—magnificent structure, magnificent view.

the stone partition that divides it into two, side-by-side openings. This arch, like Navajo Arch, is not large, but the views are absolutely grand, some of the best in the Park.

When you arrive, you will see the arch on your left and a rocky outcrop on your right. Climbing up the rocks will give you a great view of the arch. Maneuver a bit and you can get a photo of it framed by junipers. But the real treat comes when you approach the arch and look through one of the openings. There, spread out before you, is a magnificent desert landscape, stretching to the horizon.

Atop a fin on the way to Double O Arch.

Double O Arch

Return to the junction of the paths to Navajo Arch and Partition Arch and then to the main trail, which continues on flatter ground to the beginning of a fin. There, cairns direct you up onto the fin. The trail continues along the ridge for about 200 yards (180 m).

Most people seem oblivious to the narrowing of the fin as they approach the midway mark and unconscious of the increasing distance to the bottom, about fifteen feet (4.5 m) on one side and four times that on the other. They are even unconcerned about the transverse fissure near the center. They casually stop to chat or take pictures or just look around. There are some fabulous views of nearby fin formations.

Fins as seen from atop the fin shown in photo on page 103.

Double O Arch (photo by Cathy Bonan-Hamada).

Double O Arch—surprising changes in geometry as you walk around it (photo by Cathy Bonan-Hamada).

Dark Angel from Double O Arch (photo by Cathy Bonan-Hamada).

Dark Angel.

Other hikers—spineless acrophobics like the authors—wimp out and opt for the low road. Soon after you mount the fin, you come to a place on the left side where a large log has been placed against the fin near ridges that more or less suggest stairs. Using these, cowards like us can climb down and proceed on a path along the base of the fin until it rises to rejoin the main trail. There are other ways to access the low route earlier from the main trail, ways that proceed mainly on rock without threatening the fragile ecosystem of the sands. Yes, it's a route for the spineless, but even the brave and daring might do well to consider the low route when high winds rake the fins.

On the Primitive Trail near Double O Arch.

So, by one way or another, you soon find yourself at the far end of the fin. Now the path becomes steeper and rockier as it continues the short distance to Double O Arch.

And Double O it is, boasting two openings, a large one above and a much smaller one diagonally offset below. The disparity in size and the asymmetry in placement make the arch a fascinating piece of abstract sculpture. As with any good sculpture, every turn, every new angle opens surprising new perspectives. To fully appreciate Double O's intriguing geometry, you have to walk around it, climb into it, and go through it. Photographers will have a picnic. In fact, many non-photographers really do have a picnic, right there in the lower arch. Unfortunately, seating is limited, and the Park Service accepts no reservations.

Dark Angel

Find the right spot, and you can look through the lower arch and see Dark Angel, a lone column, the remnant of a collapsed fin, .25 mile (.4 km) away. Some visitors choose to hike that distance and back; it's a fairly easy walk.

Primitive Loop Trail and Private Arch

Back again at Double O (or never having left it), you can decide to return directly to the trailhead or take the Primitive Loop Trail, which eventually rejoins the main trail near Landscape Arch. The second choice adds about one mile (1.6 km) to the hike, but it rewards the hiker with interesting stretches into and out of a wash, some spectacular views of fins, and a visit to Private Arch.

The initial part of the Primitive Loop Trail, from Double O to Private Arch, is easy enough, with gentle slopes, few rocky obstacles, and no exposure worth noticing. The path crosses a wash several times and in less than a mile (1.4 km) brings you to a side trail on the right clearly marked "Private Arch." This side excursion of a few hundred yards is not to be missed. You don't see the arch from the main trail, nor from the Primitive Loop Trail, nor from the side trail leading to it, at least not until you round a bend at the very end.

Then there it is—a large opening at the base of a large and massive fin. The fin sports a tower of its own, about as impressive as the one atop Tower Arch or Turret Arch. A large, rounded slab of stone serves as a viewing platform, but it's too close to get the entire structure into camera focus without a wide-angle lens. Even with one, there's fisheye distortion to contend with. So with these excuses, we show you a photo that hardly does the arch justice.

When you return to the Primitive Loop Trail, you can go left, back to Double O Arch, and return to the Devils Garden trailhead by retracing the route you followed initially. Or you can turn right and continue on the Primitive Loop Trail to Landscape Arch. The second choice is more adventuresome, and it leads over some fairly rough terrain—rockier, hillier, and with some exposure. But for the added effort you get to see some excellent scenery.

Private Arch.

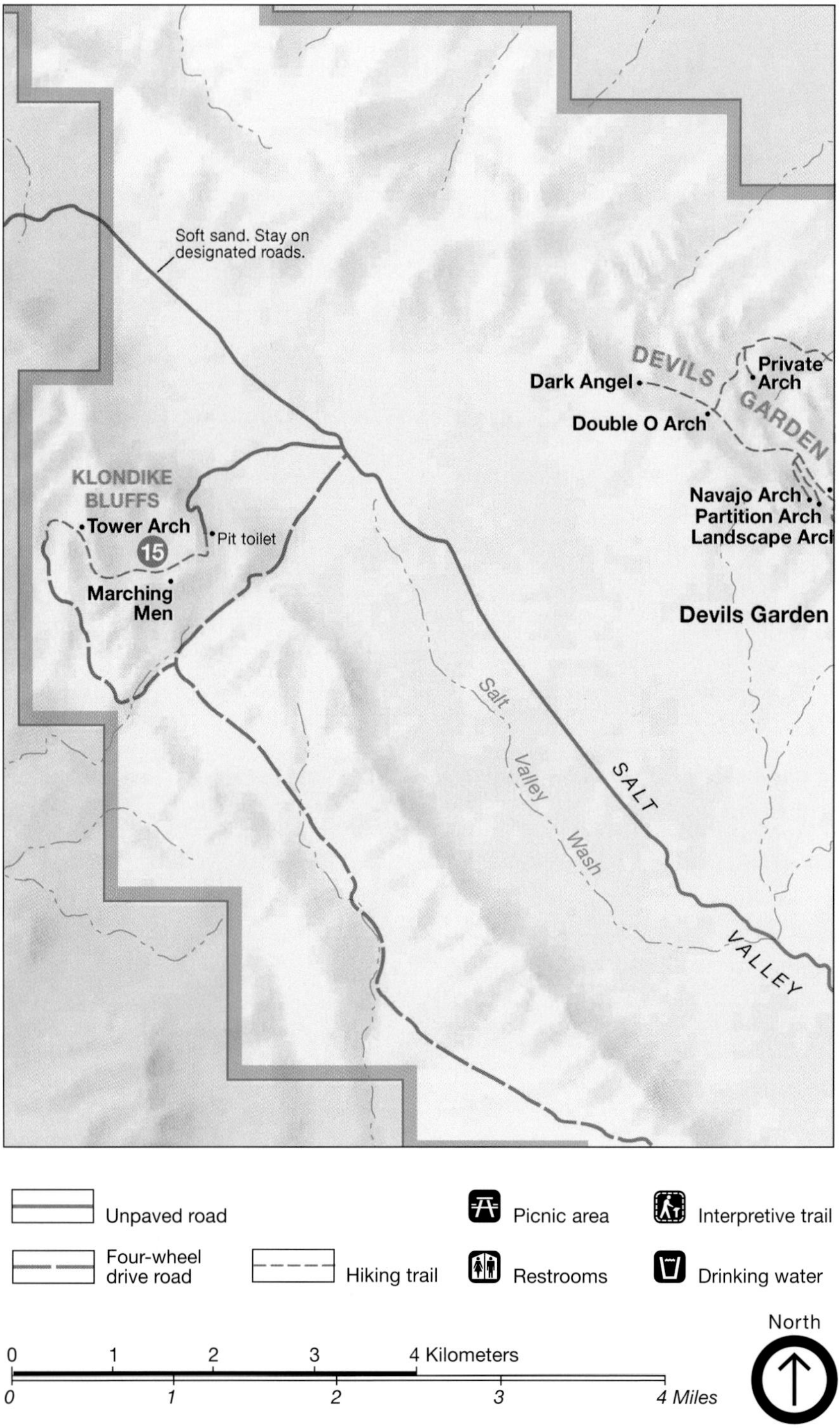

Soft sand. Stay on designated roads.
DEVILS GARDEN
Private Arch
Dark Angel
Double O Arch
KLONDIKE BLUFFS
Tower Arch
15
Pit toilet
Navajo Arch
Partition Arch
Landscape Arch
Marching Men
Devils Garden
Salt Valley Wash
SALT VALLEY
Unpaved road
Picnic area
Interpretive trail
Four-wheel drive road
Hiking trail
Restrooms
Drinking water
North
0
1
2
3
4 Kilometers
0
1
2
3
4 Miles

Klondike Bluffs, Marching Men, and Tower Arch

Trail 15

Start:	Klondike Bluffs parking area, exit east off the main road 16 miles (25.8 km) from the Visitor Center, then 9 miles (15 km) on the unpaved Salt Valley Road.
Distance:	1.7 miles (2.7 km) to Tower Arch.
Elevation gain:	Moderate.
Difficulty:	Moderate to strenuous.

Klondike Bluffs is a bit off the beaten track, and that's good, since it keeps visitation in check. Otherwise, this would be one of the most popular destinations in the Park, for here is a hike that has it all: expansive views, extraordinary rock formations, and varied terrain.

There are two roads to Klondike Bluffs, and neither is paved. Both are about nine miles (15 km) long and head west across Salt Valley. Access to the better road is described above. Mostly gravel, dirt and sand, it's barely wide enough for two-way traffic. Expect ruts and extensive sections of washboard that will give your car's shock absorbers a workout and add a touch of vibrato to your conversation. Traveling across this road after a rain is definitely not recommended. You should check the road conditions at the Visitor Center before heading out.

The other road—by far the worst way to Klondike Bluffs—is reached from the unpaved side road that leaves the main road directly across from the Balanced Rock parking area, nine miles (14.5 km) from the Visitor Center. It's a stomach-churning, kidney-pounding, alignment-wrenching, axle-breaker that's not recommended unless you have a disposable Humvee. By comparison, the better route is a superhighway.

After the long and bouncy drive to get there, you will be happy to discover that the parking area is equipped with a pit toilet. The trailhead, clearly marked, is on the perimeter of the parking loop.

As soon as you leave the parking lot, the trail ascends in earnest, rising steeply over boulders. Soon you walk out onto a long ledge, and the ascent is much gentler. A few switchbacks bring you to the top of a mesa where the terrain is nearly flat. The trail is well marked by cairns along the entire route.

To the right of the trail, Klondike Bluffs rises sharply from the floor, a compacted mass of pinnacles and fins that looks like some enormous pipe organ standing alone on a vast, deserted stage. It's worth the trip just to see this, but there is much more to come.

At some distance to the left of the trail is a massive ridge of rock jagged enough to be called a hogback. About halfway to Tower Arch, the ridge ends abruptly, to be followed by a row of stone monoliths, the Marching Men. As the monoliths decrease in size, they seem to be marching over a ridge and down the far side. It's a strange sight, even in this strange place. Again the sight is worth the trip in itself, but there is more yet to come.

The trail now becomes gradually steeper. Stone and hard-packed soil give way to fine red sand. You take one step forward and slide back down half that distance. Great fun, but a bit strenuous.

At the top of the sand hill, the trail proceeds on rock once again and crosses a low ridge. Then suddenly, you're there. Directly to your right stands Tower Arch. It's an impressive structure, its huge opening carved

Klondike Bluffs—a giant stone organ on a stage of sand.

Marching Men.

Tower Arch.

out of a massive fin ornamented on its ridge by a curious, mushroom-shaped tower. See the arch as a woman reclining on her right side. The tower is her head, and the top of the arch is her bent left leg. Could this have been the inspiration for Henry Moore's "Reclining Woman," the gigantic stone sculpture in front of the United Nations building? Probably not, but the similarity inspires the question.

The arch is so large that a wide-angle lens is needed to photograph it, since backing up will land you eight feet below in a steep-sided wash. Whatever it takes, it's an image you'll want to capture.

The trail continues for .5 mile (.8 km) to join the road from Balanced Rock, but if you choose that route, you have a long and rather dull walk along that road back to your car.

A far better option is to return by the same route that brought you to the arch. This allows you to collect the debt that the sand hill incurred on your way up. On the way down, you're owed a step-and-a-half forward progress for every step you take. And your feet also deserve some consideration. What better reward than the cushy delight of walking downhill on soft sand.

Tower Arch. →

Bibliography

Geology and History

Kiver, Eugene P., and David V. Harris, *Geology of U.S. Parklands*, 5th Ed., NY, NY: John Wiley and Sons, Inc., 1999, pp. 503–515.

Flora, Fauna and Hiking

Allen, Diane, Jeanne Treadway and Susan Kemp (editors), *Hiking Guide, Arches National Park*, Moab, UT: Published by Canyonlands Natural History Association in cooperation with the National Park Service, 1994 (out-of-print).

Eifert, Larry and Nancy Cherry Eifert, *Canyon Country Nature Guide*, Published by Larry and Nancy Cherry Eifert with cooperation and assistance from the National Park Service and Canyonlands Natural History Association.

Leach, Nicky, *Arches National Park, Where Rock Meets Sky*, Mariposa, CA: Sierra Press, 2003.

Schneider, Bill, *Best Easy Day Hikes, Canyonlands and Arches*, Guilford, CT: A Falcon Guide by The Globe Pequot Press, 1997, published in cooperation with the National Park Service, Trails Illustrated Maps, and Canyonlands Natural History Association.

Schneider, Bill, *Exploring Canyonlands and Arches National Parks*, Guilford, CT: A Falcon Guide by The Globe Pequot Press, 1996, published in cooperation with the National Park Service, Trails Illustrated Maps, and Canyonlands Natural History Association.

Taylor, Ronald J., *Sagebrush Country, A Wildflower Sanctuary*, Missoula, MT: Mountain Press Publishing Co., 1992.

Williams, David B., *A Naturalist's Guide to Canyon Country*, Guilford, CT: A Falcon Guide by The Globe Pequot Press in cooperation with Canyonlands Natural History Association, 2000.

Index

This index is limited to proper place names within Arches National Park. Entries in bold type are destinations of hikes featured in this book.

About the Authors

Jerome Malitz is the author of six books, including our best-selling *Rocky Mountain National Park Dayhiker's Guide* and the award-winning *Reflecting Nature: Garden Designs from Wild Landscapes.* He has been a professor of mathematics at the University of Colorado for the past 30 years. Additionally, he has exhibited his photography, sculpture, and paintings in several art shows. Malitz and his wife and co-author, Susan Malitz, are now completing a guidebook to Maine's Acadia National Park. They live in Boulder, Colorado.